Reel Writing

Karla Hardaway

REEL WRITING

USING MOVIES TO
TEACH THE WRITING PROCESS

KARLA HARDAWAY

CAMBRIA
PRESS

Youngstown, New York

Hardaway, Karla
        Reel Writing / Karla Hardaway
        p. cm.
        Includes bibliographical references
        ISBN10: 1-934043-01-X
        ISBN13: 978-1-934043-01-1

CHAPTER 7 THE DATING GAME

SENSE AND SENSIBILITY: IRONY AND SATIRE 107

CHAPTER 8 STORY EVOLUTION

COMPARISON AND CONTRAST ESSAY 119

CHAPTER 9 SHORT ORDER STORY

FRIED GREEN TOMATOES: VIGNETTES AND FRAME STORY 125

CHAPTER 10 LIFE ROAD TRIP

RIDING IN CARS WITH BOYS: MEMOIRS 139

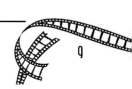

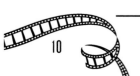

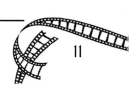

WHY USE THIS BOOK?

Everyone wants higher test scores—parents, students, administrators, politicians. Most people believe that returning to the "basics" will achieve higher scores. However, students seem to be reading—and writing—less and less. They spend their time watching television, playing video games, and watching movies.

Research shows that reading and writing skills are inherently linked. Reading is decoding; writing is encoding. The two processes require almost the same cognitive process. If a student improves his reading skills, his writing skills improve; if a student improves his writing skills, his reading skills improve. The trick is to get students to write more—and to enjoy it.

As a veteran English, speech, and creative writing teacher of thirty-one years, I have seen first hand the transforming power of drama and writing activities on students' learning. My role as an educator has changed through the years from "giver of knowledge" to "learning coach." When students write and share their writing, it comes alive. As they begin to write, they appreciate the work of other writers. As they interpret and perform writing, they learn the power of language to communicate and record their lives. Movies are the vanguard for the most current writing trends and the reflection of the values of society. Why not use movies to draw students into the exciting world of writing and self-expression?

I have tried to include movies that students will actually like without much prodding and which are appropriate for high school. Many colleges teach similar film courses using films such as *Apocalypse Now*, *The Graduate*, *Full Metal Jacket*, etc. These films contain subject matter or language which is inappropriate for high school students. Some college courses use "oldies" like *Casablanca, Mr. Smith goes to Washington,* and *Citizen*

Kane, but I find that students tend to "glaze over" when watching old black and white movies. And besides, if students will study these films in college, why not introduce them to additional movies in high school? Most college courses also emphasize film techniques and film history; *Reel Writing* uses movies to teach literary concepts and writing. My objective is to help teachers motivate students to write by using more current movies and classics which are often over-looked in high school courses.

Teachers are busy people. We have little time to develop new teaching materials. As a veteran teacher myself, I am always grateful for easy-to-use materials to supplement my classroom instruction. Middle-school teachers will be able to use the book, as well, as long as they are careful to select the movies appropriate for their age group.

HOW TO USE THIS BOOK

Reel Writing is actually designed as a text to be used in a writing intensive course taught on a four by four block. It can easily be adapted to a traditional fifty-minute period class or as supplementary material in any English course. The movie units can be taught in order or pulled out as separate units to supplement standard classroom curriculum.

Literature concepts are taught through the medium of film. Students are taught to "read" movies using the same skills needed for reading literature. Each unit uses a movie to teach a literary concept. Course information such as definitions, history, cast lists, etc., is included for each unit. Teachers are given various activities for introducing literary concepts. Pages are ready to be reproduced to hand out to students or to make overhead transparencies. A viewing guide is included for each movie to be filled out as students watch the movie or as a comprehension check at the end of the movie. Students complete pre-viewing exercises, view the film, and then respond to the film through quizzes, oral assignments, group activities and performances, or writing assignments. Students write individually and in groups. They write character sketches, short stories, film reviews, skits, essays, term papers, and poetry (songs).

Each movie unit contains the following information to help the teacher in planning:

Objectives: A list of concepts and skills the students will learn.
Notes to the Teacher: A summary of the movie, its rating, and the length.
Possible Problems: Any information the teacher needs to know to avoid problems.
Procedures: An outline of the exercises, information, viewing guides, quizzes, writing or group assignments, and rubrics.

MATERIALS NEEDED

Obviously you will need copies of the movies to show either in video tape or DVD format. You will also need the appropriate VCR or DVD player. The "Fair Use"copyright laws allow teachers to use videos in the classroom so long as the videos are used for instruction and not for entertainment. For detailed information, see <http://www

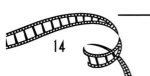

.mediafestival.org/copyrightchart.html.>. You may show videos which are obtained legally—purchased, rented, borrowed, or checked out of the library.

You may want to invest in a censoring device such as a *Guardian TV* or *Protect TV*, depending on your school district policies. These devices filter out profanity by "reading" the subtitles. My students, however, do not like the devices because they tend to filter out whole lines of dialogue instead of single words.

The materials in the book are designed for photocopying or making transparencies.

ABOUT THE AUTHOR

Karla Hardaway has a master's degree in education and has been teaching English, speech, debate, and creative writing in Louisiana for more than thirty years. She has taught English at every grade level from grades seven through twelve. She is currently teaching sophomore English, creative writing, and Film as Literature at Parkway High School in Bossier City, Louisiana.

She is very active in training new teachers and implementing new teaching methods. She has mentored eleven new teachers through Louisiana's assessment program and has trained eleven student teachers from two state colleges. She recently served on a committee to develop Louisiana's new comprehensive curriculum which was implemented in 2005. She helped write the curriculum for Louisiana's new STAR program (Students Teaching and Reaching), a course which encourages high school students to enter the teaching profession.

Mrs. Hardaway is the mother of four children and currently resides in Shreveport, Louisiana, with her husband Steven Hardaway.

FILM AS LITERATURE CLASS

Parents,

The *Film as Literature* class is really a writing intensive course that is designed to improve student writing and reading skills. Literature concepts are taught through the medium of film. Students must view the movies in class in order to complete the writing and group projects. If a student misses class, he must secure the movies on his own to view (most can easily be rented and many may already be owned by the student). The basic concepts of the class are described and a list of movies is included. If you have questions, please call me at _____ or email me at _____. All of these movies are rated PG13, PG, or G, or they are edited to secure that rating. Students may choose their own movies for some of the out-of-class assignments so long as they meet your approval.

_____
Teacher

Course Structure:

Each class period will begin with a free write, a learning log question, a response to a quote, or a word of the day for the first five activity.

Each new literary concept and movie will take approximately 1-1/2 weeks to teach. Students learn the new concept, do some type of pre-viewing activity, view the movie and complete a viewing guide, take a quiz over the concept and movie guide, and then do some type of writing assignment or group project to present to the class.

Students will also complete assignments outside of class in writing, research, reading and critiquing other movies or television shows, reading novels, etc.

Course Outline:

Elements of Plot—*Spiderman*
Plot with hook resolution—*Jumanji*
Characterization—*Anne of Green Gables*
Symbolism—*Places in the Heart*
Universal Theme—*Miracle on Thirty-fourth Street*
Setting—*Last of the Mohicans*
Irony-Satire—*Sense and Sensibility*
Compare/contrast Essay—Students read a book which has been made into a movie, view the movie at home, and write a comparison/contrast essay.
Vignettes—*Fried Green Tomatoes*
Memoirs—*Riding in Cars with Boys*

Historical Movies—*Hawaii*
Research Project—Students view a historical movie outside of class and then research the historical validity of the movie and write a paper.
Accepting Others—*Radio*
Stereotypes—*Never Been Kissed*
Revised Fairytale—*Ever After*
Allusions—*Big Fish*
Jargon—*Pirates of the Caribbean*
Hollywood Classics—*War of the Worlds*
Realism—*Grapes of Wrath*
Classical Musical—*Singing in the Rain*

I have read and understand this information.

_____   _____
Student   Date   Parent or Guardian   Date

Name _____

FILM INVENTORY

You have elected to take a *Responding to Film as Literature* class. I would like to get some idea of your expectation your likes, and your dislikes. Please answer the following questions:

1. Who is your favorite actor or actress? Why do you like this person? What are some of the movies in which he/she has starred?

2. What are your movie preferences? Rank each from 1-5, with 5 being most liked and 1 being the least liked.

Romance	1	2	3	4	5	Animated	1	2	3	4	5
War	1	2	3	4	5	Crime	1	2	3	4	5
Action/adventure	1	2	3	4	5	Family	1	2	3	4	5
Horror	1	2	3	4	5	Sci-Fi	1	2	3	4	5
Comedy	1	2	3	4	5	Musical	1	2	3	4	5

3. Name three movies which you really enjoyed and give at least one reason why you enjoyed each.

4. Upon what do you base your decision to see a movie?

5. What is your purpose in taking this class?

6. What percentage of class time would you like to spend on each of the following activities? Your numbers should add up to 100%.

_____Viewing films   _____Working in groups

_____Researching background information   _____Discussing films

_____Writing stories, essays, papers   _____Performing skits and group activities

                                                                         _____Other

 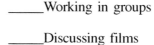

Name _____

MOVIE INTERNET SCAVENGER HUNT

Go to this web address: <http://www.imdb.com/>. This is the Internet Movie Database (IMDB). This is one of the best internet resources available for movie information. Answer the following questions:

1. Click on *Tops at the Box Office*. What is currently the most popular movie in the United States?

2. How much money has this movie made?

3. Summarize this movie in one sentence.

4. Find a movie in the *Weekend Box-office Summary* which you have seen. What is the title? Under what genre is it listed?

5. Read some of the user comments. What seems to be viewers' opinions of the movie?

6. Go back to the main page. Click on the *All-Time Box Office*. What are the top ten grossing movies in US history? How much money did each make?

7. What number is *The Sixth Sense* in the *All-Time Box Office* list?

8. Go back to the main page. What is the top rated family title?

9. What is the top rated male movie?

10. Go to *Search*. Look up *The Shawshank Redemption*. In what year was this movie made?

11. Who are three of the main actors in this movie?

12. Who wrote the screenplay?

REEL WRITING

MOVIE INTERNET SCAVENGER HUNT PAGE 2

13. Describe one of the "goofs" made in *Shawshank.*

14. Copy down the first quote listed which was made by Captain Hadley.

15. Now search for one of your favorite movies. Read what other IMDB users think about this movie and summarize. Write down the name of the movie and say whether or not you agree with them.

16. I want to see a movie but I can't remember the title. I know one of the main characters is named Clarice Starling. What is the name of the movie?

17. Look for a movie in which John Wayne starred. In what year did John Wayne die?

18. Go to the *Browse* section. Find some interesting trivia about a crazy credit and write it down.

19. Now go to this web address: <http/www.script-o-rama.com/snazzy/dircut.html>. What is the opening sentence of the *Nightmare Before Christmas*?

20. Find the opening line of a movie you like. Name the movie and write the line.

21. Now go to this web address: <http://dir.yahoo.com/Entertainment/Movies_and_Film/Trivia/Quizzes/>. Take the quiz *Where Have I Seen That Guy*? What was your score?

LITERARY TERMS PRE-TEST

Define each of the following words. Explain what the term means in relation to literature and films. This is only a pre-test to determine your current level of understanding. Do your best!

1. indirect characterization

2. basic situation

3. rising action

4. climax

5. denouement/resolution

6. internal conflict

7. external conflict

8. symbolism

9. hook resolution

10. direct characterization

11. theme

12. satire

13. thesis sentence

14. frame story

15. rhetorical question

16. setting

17. memoirs

18. anecdote

19. proverb

20. verbal irony

21. situational irony

22. dramatic irony

23. metaphor

24. allusion

25. vignette

26. disability

27. flashback

28. stereotype

29. swashbuckler

30. genre

31. realism

32. jargon

33. imagery

34. suspense

35. catalogue musical

36. dialogue tag

37. politically correct

38. plot

LITERARY TERMS PRE-TEST—TEACHER

Define each of the following words. Explain what the term means in relation to literature and films. This is only a pre-test to determine your current level of understanding. Do your best!

1. **indirect characterization**—The audience/reader determines what a character is like through appearance, speech, actions, and interaction of other characters.
2. **basic situation**—The introduction of the setting, characters, and conflict.
3. **rising action**—Complications of conflict which create suspense.
4. **climax**—The highest point of excitement in a story and the point at which the winner of the conflict is obvious.
5. **denouement/resolution**—The falling action of a story; the conclusion; the part of the story where the loose ends are tied up.
6. **internal conflict**—The character is struggling with a decision, values, emotions, etc. within himself.
7. **external conflict**—The character is struggling with a force outside himself such as nature, man, machine, society, supernatural, etc.
8. **symbolism**—A person , place, thing, or event stands for both itself and for something beyond itself.
9. **hook resolution**—The resolution is not completely resolved and the action may even begin rising again.
10. **direct characterization**—The author tells the audience/reader directly what a character is like or is thinking.
11. **theme**—The central idea or insight revealed by a work of literature.
12. **satire**— The use of ridicule to criticize folly or vice.
13. **thesis sentence**—The central idea of an essay, usually found at the end of the introduction and the beginning of the conclusion.
14. **frame story**—The outer story which includes flashbacks to an inner story or stories.
15. **rhetorical question**—A question used to gain attention in a speech or story.
16. **setting**—The time and place of a story.
17. **memoirs**—A piece of autobiographical writing, usually shorter in length than an autobiography. The memoir captures certain moments, events, or highlights of a person's life.
18. **anecdote**—a short narrative used to make a point.
19. **proverb**—A saying which teaches a truth.
20. **verbal irony**— the meaning intended by the speaker is not what the words actually convey; may be sarcasm.
21. **situational irony**—The end of the story is different from what the audience/reader expects.
22. **dramatic irony**—The audience/reader knows something a character in the story does not know or a character in the story knows something another character does not know.
23. **metaphor**—A figure of speech that makes a comparison between two unlike things wighout using a connective word.
24. **allusion**— a reference to a famous person, place, thing, or part of another work of literature.
25. **vignette**— a brief sketch, narrative, or short-short story. It may be a separate whole or a portion of a larger work.
26. **disability**—a physical or mental handicap.
27. **flashback**—A scene that interrupts the present action of the plot to show events that happened at an earlier time.
28. **stereotype**—A character which is labeled into a category. This label may be based on such characteristics as clothing, looks, speech, actions, or group association.
29. **swashbuckler**—A pirate.
30. **genre**— A category of literature, marked by a distinctive style, form, or content.
31. **realism**— the practice of presenting life exactly as it is. No attempt is made to glamorize it.
32. **jargon**— language which is characteristic to a particular group. Jargon may be associated with sports, computer language, teacher terminology, medical terminology, citizen band radios, etc.
33. **imagery**—Language that appeals to the senses.
34. **suspense**—The uncertainty or anxiety we feel about what is going to happen next.
35. **catalogue musical**—A musical used as a medium to showcase a list of songs which were already written.
36. **dialogue tag**—The portion of written dialogue which includes the *he said* part.
37. **politically correct**—The use of euphemisms to avoid offending anyone.
38. **plot**—The structure of a story which includes the basic situation, rising action, climax, and denouement.

Name _____

REVIEW SHEET FOR FINAL

Define each of the following words:

1. basic situation
2. internal conflict
3. external conflict
4. rising action
5. climax
6. denouement/resolution
7. hook resolution
8. direct characterization
9. indirect characterization
10. dialogue tag
11. theme
12. thesis sentence
13. rhetorical question
14. anecdote
15. symbolism
16. continuity error
17. setting as character
18. setting
19. satire
20. verbal irony

21. situational irony
22. dramatic irony
23. sense or sensibility
24. frame story
25. vignette
26. flashback
27. Dear John letter
28. Works Cited page
29. disability
30. stereotype
31. fairy tale
32. politically correct
33. allusion
34. fish story
35. swashbuckler
36. jargon
37. memoirs
38. proverb
39. plot
40. suspense

Know basic plot of each movie. Know theme of some. Know allusions in *Big Fish*. Know symbolism in some. Know irony in some.

REEL WRITING

Name _____

FINAL FOR RESPONDING TO FILM AS LITERATURE

Matching: Match each term to its best description.

A. basic situation
B. hook resolution
C. direct characterization
D. dialogue tag
E. theme
AB. anecdote
AC. symbolism
AD. continuity error
AE. setting
BC. satire
BD. climax
BE. rhetorical question
CD. internal conflict
CE. verbal irony
ABC. denouement

1. The point in the story in which the winner of the conflict becomes obvious.
2. The introduction of the characters, setting, and conflict.
3. The character is struggling with some important decision.
4. An object is used to stand for a larger idea.
5. A method to gain interest in a speech or essay. No answer is expected.
6. Identifies who the speaker is.
7. The time and place.
8. A character says the opposite of what he really means.
9. The underlying truth taught by a story.
10. The conclusion of a story.
11. An interesting story used to gain attention or make a point.
12. The author explicitly tells the reader/audience about a character.
13. Makes fun of something to make a point.
14. The end leaves the reader/audience hanging.
15. There is some flaw in the filming of a movie.

Matching: Match each term to its best description.

A. thesis sentence
B. setting as character
C. situational irony
D. dramatic irony
E. frame story
AB. flashback
AC. Dear John letter
AE. Works Cited page
BC. stereotype
BD. allusion
BE. fish story
CD. swashbuckler
CE. jargon
ABC. memoirs
BCD. vignette

16. The end is different from what the audience expects.
17. The time and place are important in driving the plot.
18. The core statement of an essay.
19. A large story which begins in the present and then flashes back in time to tell an inner story.
20. A label assigned to a group of people based on appearance, education, age, etc.
21. A reference in literature to another work of literature.
22. An exaggerated story.
23. The recorded story of a person's life told by that person.
24. A short story which is complete by itself but is usually connected to several like stories through a frame story.
25. A particular kind of speech used by a particular profession, sport, hobby group, etc.
26. Written when someone wants to break up a relationship.
27. The audience or some characters know something other characters do not know.
28. The story begins in the present and then goes back in time.
29. Gives credit to the writer of the information.
30. A pirate.

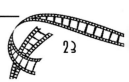

FINAL FOR RESPONDING TO FILM AS LITERATURE PAGE 2

Multiple Choice

31. The climax of *Spiderman* is A) when Peter tells MJ that he doesn't love her, B) when the Green Goblin is killed by Spiderman, C) when Peter discovers that his friend is dating MJ.

32. The climax of *War of the Worlds* is A) when the creatures begin to die, B) when Ray finds his son alive, C) when an airplane falls on the house.

33. The climax of *Jumanji* is A) when the objects go back into the board, B) when Alan throws the game into the river, C) when the children show up at the Christmas party.

34. The idea of everyone's getting along is symbolized in *Places in the Heart* by A) the fact that Moses leaves to protect Edna's family, B) the communion scene at the end of the movie, C) the blind man helps cook meals.

35. *The Last of the Mohicans* gets its title from the fact that A) all the Mohican tribe is killed, B) the father and adopted son are the only ones left, C) the Mohicans are defeated by the British.

36. The resolution of *Pirates of the Caribbean* is when A) the commodore is going to hang Will, B) the treasure is restored, C) Elizabeth saves Will and Captain Sparrow's lives.

37. The resolution of *Riding in Cars with Boys* is when A) the main character is embarrassed at the party, B) she decides to marry Ray, C) her son gets Ray to sign the paper.

38. The resolution of *Ever After* begins when A) the stepmother and stepsister are made to be servants, B) the prince decides not to marry the Spanish woman, C) the artist makes Cinderella into a beauty.

Matching: Allusions

39. spiders, tree branches, bees	A. Karl and Ed
40. Spector	B. Ed buys back Spector
41. baptism	C. The Garden of Eden
42. redemption of mankind	D. The Road Not Taken
43. David and Goliath	E. Ed dies and lives again

Matching: Theme

44. *Miracle on 34th Street*	A. A person's stories reveal his personality.
45. *Places in the Heart*	B. We should value all human beings.
46. *Radio*	C. Even the little things can be very important.
47. *Spiderman*	D. All people live on in our memories.
48. *Big Fish*	E. We should all believe like little children.
49. *Ever After*	AB. With great power comes great responsibility.
50. *War of the Worlds*	AC. True love wins in the end.

EVALUATION OF FILM CLASS

These are the movies we watched. Please rate them by degree of enjoyment with one being the least enjoyed and five being very much enjoyed.

Spiderman	1	2	3	4	5
Jumanji	1	2	3	4	5
Anne of Green Gables	1	2	3	4	5
Places in the Heart	1	2	3	4	5
Miracle on Thirty-fourth Street	1	2	3	4	5
Last of the Mohicans	1	2	3	4	5
Sense and Sensibility	1	2	3	4	5
Fried Green Tomatoes	1	2	3	4	5
Riding in Cars with Boys	1	2	3	4	5
Hawaii	1	2	3	4	5
Radio	1	2	3	4	5
Never Been Kissed	1	2	3	4	5
Ever After	1	2	3	4	5
Big Fish	1	2	3	4	5
Pirates of the Caribbean	1	2	3	4	5
War of the Worlds	1	2	3	4	5
Grapes of Wrath	1	2	3	4	5
Singin" in the Rain	1	2	3	4	5

1. Name at least four things you learned in this course which you didn't know before.

2. What did you think of the viewing guides? Explain.

3. Which movie did you like the best? Why?

4. Which movie did you like the least? Why?

5. Which group activities did you like the most? Do you have any suggestions to improve them?

6. Which writing activities did you like the most? Do you have any suggestions to improve them?

7. What can I do to improve this class?

8. Can you suggest any other movies which I might include in the class? What concept could each be used to teach?

9. Would you recommend this class to another student? What would you say about it?

chapter 1
Weave a Tangled Web
Spiderman: Elements of Plot

OBJECTIVES

- Students will learn the basic plot elements present in most short stories and be able to identify them in works of fiction.
- Students will use the basic plot elements to write a story and perform a skit.
- Students will become critical viewers who notice details.
- Students will practice public speaking skills and listening skills.

NOTES TO THE TEACHER

Spiderman is a fast-paced story which easily holds students' attention. Peter Parker is bitten by a spider and then develops supernatural powers. Dr. Osborn does a science experiment and also develops supernatural powers. Peter wrestles with the moral dilemma of how to use his new powers, for good or evil purposes.

Spiderman is rated PG-13 For stylized violence and action and is 121 minutes long.

POSSIBLE PROBLEMS

None.

PROCEDURES

1. **Plot Elements of a Story**—Make transparencies. Have students copy the information as notes and answer any questions.

2. **Plot Diagram**—Use this sheet to give students a visual picture of a short story.

3. **Round-Robin Stories**—Divide students into groups of four. Have students write round-robin stories and share the stories with the class.

4. *Spiderman* **Comics Origin**—Share this information with the students <http://www.angelfire.com/mo/ SpidermanVenom/Spiderman.html> and encourage them to bring in memorabilia and pictures to share with the class. You will find an abundance of calendars, comic books, clothing, etc.

5. **Continuity Errors**—Direct students to the Internet Movie Data Base <http://www.imdb.com/> to find a list of continuity errors and familiar quotes about *Spiderman*. They should have this list available during the viewing of the movie in order to try to find as many as possible in the movie.

6. *Spiderman* **Viewing Guide**—Students answer these questions as they watch the movie.

7. **Plot Elements Group Script And Rubric**—Divide the class into groups and have them write a script to perform which contains all the plot elements. Use this rubric to assign a grade to each group's performance.

8. **Plot Elements of Movie of Choice**—This handout is to be used for a homework assignment.

PLOT ELEMENTS OF A STORY

Basic situation (exposition)—The introduction of the story. Reader is introduced to the character/characters, setting, and conflict.

Complications/conflicts—Struggles encountered by the main character. May be internal or external.

Climax—The highest point of excitement in the story. The point at which the winner of the conflict is determined.

Resolution (denouement)—The conclusion of the story; the falling action. The loose ends are tied up. The story feels finished.

TYPES OF CONFLICT

Internal conflict — man verses himself. A character might deal with finding values; setting priorities; dealing with strong emotions such as love, hate, revenge, jealousy; instincts; etc.

External conflict — Man vs. man
Man vs. society
Man vs. machine
Man vs. nature
Man vs. supernatural
Man vs. deity

Plot Diagram

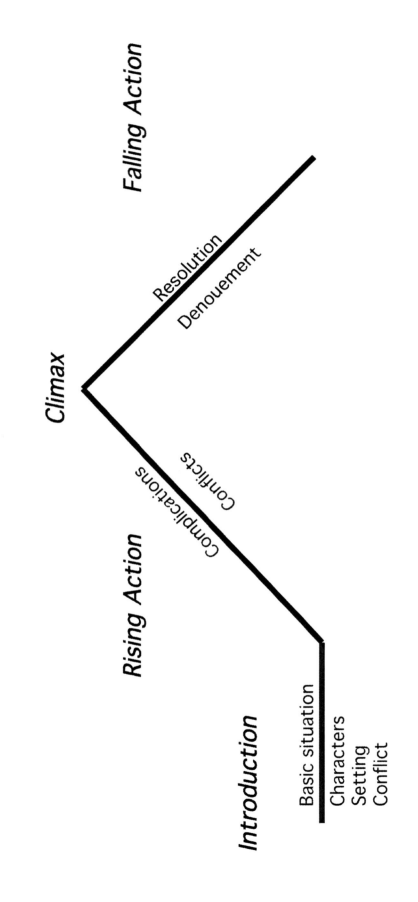

Falling Action

Resolution

Denouement

Climax

Rising Action

Complications

Conflicts

Introduction

Basic situation

Characters
Setting
Conflict

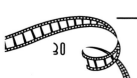

ROUND-ROBIN STORIES

1. You will divided into groups of four. Each person is to write the basic situation of a story. Then you will pass your paper to the person on your left.

2. When you receive the story from the person on your right, you will then add the rising action.

3. Now everyone trades papers again and adds the climax.

4. Now everyone trades papers again and adds the resolution/denouement.

5. Now give the paper back to the original owner and let each person read his finished story to the entire class.

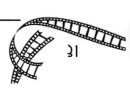

Name _____

SPIDERMAN VIEWING GUIDE

Briefly identify these characters as you watch the movie:

1. Tobey Maguire ... Spiderman/Peter Parker—

2. William Dafoe ... Green Goblin/Norman Osborn—

3. Kirsten Dunst ... Mary Jane Watson—

4. James Franco ...Harry Osborn—

5. Cliff Robertson ... Ben Parker—

6. Rosemary Harris ... May Parker—

7. J.K. Simmons ... Jonah Jameson—

8. Joe Manganiello ... Flash—

Answer the following questions as you watch the movie:

1. What "line" does Harry steal from Peter to impress Mary Jane?

2. How does Peter begin to talk to Mary Jane on the field trip?

3. What happens which causes Peter to get supernatural powers?

4. With whom does Peter live?

5. What does Dr. Osborn do which gives him supernatural powers?

6. Who lives next door to Peter?

7. Whom does Dr. Osborn kill?

8. Why does Flash fight with Peter at school?

9. Describe Peter's new powers.

Name _____

SPIDERMAN VIEWING GUIDE PAGE 2

10. Why do MJ and Peter go into their back yards?

11. What do MJ and Peter want to become when they grow up?

12. Who talks to Peter about changing into a man?

13. How much will the winner of the prize fight get?

14. How does Uncle Ben die?

15. In what grade were Peter, Mary Jane, and Harry?

16. What job does MJ get in the city?

17. Who does MJ say she is going out with?

18. Why was Peter fired from his delivery job?

19. How much does Peter make from his first set of photos?

20. Where does Norman see the Green Goblin?

21. How does the Green Goblin put Spiderman to sleep?

22. What does the Green Goblin want Spiderman to do?

23. How does MJ thank Spiderman for saving her?

24. Who was in the burning building?

25. How does Norman know Peter is Spiderman?

26. Who does MJ say she is really in love with?

27. Spiderman has to choose between which two people to save?

28. How does the Green Goblin die?

29. What does Harry vow to do about Spiderman?

30. Why won't Peter say he loves MJ?

Name _____

SPIDERMAN VIEWING GUIDE PAGE 3

Discussion questions: Answer these questions after the movie. Use complete sentences.

1. What is the basic situation of *Spiderman?*

2. What is the major conflict of the movie?

3. What point is the climax?

4. What happens in the denouement?

5. Uncle Ben says, "With great power comes great responsibility." Do you think Peter is accurate or extreme in applying this saying to his own life? Explain.

6. Do you blame Harry for wanting to kill Spiderman? Why or why not?

SPIDERMAN VIEWING GUIDE—TEACHER

Briefly identify these characters as you watch the movie:

1. Tobey Maguire ... Spiderman/Peter Parker—

2. William Dafoe ... Green Goblin/Norman Osborn—

3. Kirsten Dunst ... Mary Jane Watson—

4. James Franco ... Harry Osborn—

5. Cliff Robertson ... Ben Parker—

6. Rosemary Harris ... May Parker—

7. J.K. Simmons ... Jonah Jameson—

8. Joe Manganiello ... Flash—

Answer the following questions as you watch the movie:

1. What "line" does Harry steal from Peter to impress Mary Jane? Blend to the enviroment.

2. How does Peter begin to talk to Mary Jane on the field trip? Asks to take her picture.

3. What happens which causes Peter get supernatural powers? Spider bite.

3. With whom does Peter live? Uncle Ben and Aunt May.

5. What does Dr. Osborn do which gives him supernatural powers? Drinks a potient.

6. Who lives next door to Peter? Mary Jane.

7. Whom does Dr. Osborn kill? His lab assistant.

8. Why does Flash fight with Peter at school? Food tray hits him.

9. Describe Peter's new powers. Shoots a web, can jump high, can hear well.

10. Why do MJ and Peter go into their back yards? MJ's parents are fighting and Peter is taking out the trash.

11. What do MJ and Peter want to become when they grow up? Photographer and actress.

12. Who talks to Peter about changing into a man? Uncle Ben.

13. How much will the winner of the prize fight get? $3,000.

14. How does Uncle Ben die? Car-jacker shoots him.

15. In what grade were Peter, Mary Jane, and Harry? 12th.

16. What job does MJ get in the city? Waitress.

17. Who does MJ say she is going out with? Harry.

18. Why was Peter fired from his delivery job? Late to work.

19. How much does Peter make from his first set of photos? $300.

20. Where does Norman see the Green Goblin? In the mirror.

21. How does the Green Goblin put Spiderman to sleep? Green gas.

22. What does the Green Goblin want Spiderman to do? Join him.

23. How does MJ thank Spiderman for saving her? Upside down kiss.

24. Who was in the burning building? Green Goblin.

25. How does Norman know Peter is Spiderman? Peter's arm is bleeding.

26. Who does MJ say she is really in love with? Spiderman.

27. Spiderman has to choose between which two people to save? MJ or the kids.

28. How does the Green Goblin die? Stabbed by his Goblin Glider.

29. What does Harry vow to do about Spiderman? Make him pay.

30. Why won't Peter say he loves MJ? Wants to protect her.

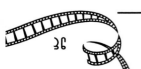

Discussion questions: Answer these questions after the movie. Use complete sentences.

1. What is the basic situation of *Spiderman?*

2. What is the major conflict of the movie?

3. What point is the climax?

4. What happens in the denouement?

5. Uncle Ben says, "With great power comes great responsibility." Do you think Peter is accurate or extreme in applying this saying to his own life? Explain.

6. Do you blame Harry for wanting to kill Spiderman? Why or why not?

Name _____

PLOT ELEMENTS GROUP SCRIPT AND RUBRIC

You will be divided into groups of four or five students. You must write a script to perform which includes all the parts of the plot diagram: basic situation, rising action, climax, and resolution.

Each person in the group must have a part to perform. The conflict must be developed adequately. A neatly written script must be handed in to the teacher.

Names of people in group:

ELEMENTS	**W**eak (4 pts.)	**A**verage (6 pts.)	**G**ood (8 pts.)	**E**xcellent (10 pts.)
Basic Situation—Characters Introduced				
Setting Introduced				
Conflict Introduced				
Complications/ Conflict Developed				
Climax				
Resolution				
Effort				
Written Text				

Total Points: ____/80

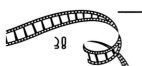

REEL WRITING

Name _____

PLOT ELEMENTS OF MOVIE OF CHOICE

Choose a movie or a television show which tells a story. Summarize the parts of the plot in the sections below:

1. Basic situation—

2. Rising action—

3. Climax—

4. Falling action—

chapter 2

It Just Never Ends,
Does It?

Jumanji: Plot With a
Hook Resolution

OBJECTIVES

- Students will review the basic plot elements of a story.
- Students will be able to identify a resolution which ends with a "hook."
- Students will write stories which contain hook resolutions.
- Students will become critical viewers who notice details.

NOTES TO THE TEACHER

Jumanji is a story about a boy who discovers a magical game at a construction site. He and his girlfriend begin to play the game until he is sucked into the game. Years later, two other children, Judy and Peter, find the game in the attic and begin to play.

Jumanji is rated PG for menacing fantasy action and some mild language and is 103 minutes long.

POSSIBLE PROBLEMS

Some parents might object to the use of magic in literature.

PROCEDURES

1. **Free Write**—Students write for ten minutes on the following topic to introduce *Jumanji*: A magic _____.

2. **Write the Resolution**—Chose a short story with which you are familiar and read it aloud to your class. Stop at the point of the climax and ask students to write their own endings to the story. I like to use a story called "Dear John" in Carl Reiner's book *How Paul Robeson Saved My Life*.

   Have students read their own endings aloud and then read the real ending. Talk about why some writers stop short of the complete resolution in storytelling. Tell them that these kinds of stories have "hook" resolutions. The purpose of hook resolutions is to involve the reader in the outcome or possibly to leave room for a sequel.

3. **Continuity Errors**—Have students access the Internet Movie Data Base <http://www.imdb.com/> to find a list of continuity errors in *Jumanji*. They should have this list available during the viewing of the movie in order to try to find as many as possible in the movie.

4. ***Jumanji* Viewing Guide**—Students answer these questions as they watch the movie.

5. **Hook Resolution Stories**—Students construct short stories which include all plot elements but have a hook resolution.

6. **Hook Resolution Story Rubric**—Use this rubric to assign grades to the students' stories

Name _____

JUMANJI VIEWING GUIDE

Briefly identify these characters as you watch the movie:

1. Robin Williams .... Alan Parrish—

2. Jonathan Hyde .... Samuel Alan Parrish/Hunter Van Pelt—

3. Kirsten Dunst .... Judy Shepherd—

4. Bradley Pierce .... Peter Shepherd—

5. Bonnie Hunt .... Sarah Whittle—

6. Bebe Neuwirth .... Aunt Nora Shepherd—

7. David Alan Grier .... Carl Bentley—

Answer these questions as you watch the movie:

1. In what year does the movie open?

2. What gets cut up on the conveyer belt at the factory?

3. Why does Alan Parish hide in the shoe factory?

4. What do Alan and his father argue about at dinner?

5. How much time passes after the argument and the next part of the movie?

6. What does Peter see in the attic which frightens him?

7. With whom do the children Judy and Peter live?

8. "A tiny bite will make you itch" causes what to come out of the game?

9. What appears in the kitchen?

10. What will make the game end?

11. Where are Peter and Judy's parents?

12. Whose turn is it after Judy?

13. What do people say happened to Alan Parish?

14. The thunder is really what?

15. What did the pelican steal?

Name _____

JUMANJI VIEWING GUIDE PAGE 2

16. Who says, "You're not a postal worker, are you?"

17. How does Peter save the game from the river?

18. What did "A law of Jumanji having been broken, you will sit back even more than your token" mean?

19. Why does Peter begin to change to a monkey?

20. Who was Carl Bentley twenty-six years ago?

21. How does the hunter get paint on his clothes?

22. What causes the aunt to wreck her car?

23. Why does Alan tear Peter's pants?

24. How does Carl finally lose his car?

25. What animal appears during the monsoon?

26. Whose turn ends the game?

27. What do Sarah and Alan do with the game?

28. How does the "game" continue to be alive?

Discussion questions: Answer these questions after the movie. Use complete sentences.

1. What does this movie seem to say about events which happen on a continuum in time? Do you agree or disagree with this theory?

2. Do you think *Jumanji* is suitable viewing for young children? Explain.

3. Describe three of the curses which occurred during the game.

4. Explain the "hook" resolution of *Jumanji*.

JUMANJI VIEWING GUIDE—TEACHER

Briefly identify these characters as you watch the movie:

1. Robin Williams .... Alan Parrish—

2. Jonathan Hyde .... Samuel Alan Parrish/Hunter Van Pelt—

3. Kirsten Dunst .... Judy Shepherd—

4. Bradley Pierce .... Peter Shepherd—

5. Bonnie Hunt .... Sarah Whittle—

6. Bebe Neuwirth .... Aunt Nora Shepherd—

7. David Alan Grier .... Carl Bentley—

Answer these questions as you watch the movie:

1. In what year does the movie open? 1869.

2. What gets cut up on the conveyer belt at the factory? Carl's shoe.

3. Why does Alan Parish hide in the shoe factory? Kids on bikes are chasing him.

4. What do Alan and his father argue about at dinner? Boarding school.

5. How much time passes after the argument and the next part of the movie? 26 years.

6. What does Peter see in the attic which frightens him? Bat.

7. With whom do the children Judy and Peter live? Aunt Nora.

8. "A tiny bite will make you itch" causes what to come out of the game? Mosquito.

9. What appears in the kitchen? Monkeys.

10. What will make the game end? Reach Jumanji and call out its name.

11. Where are Peter and Judy's parents? They died.

12. Whose turn is it after Judy? Sarah Whittle.

13. What do people say happened to Alan Parish? His father murdered him and chopped him into little pieces.

14. The thunder is really what? A stampede.

JUMANJI VIEWING GUIDE—TEACHER PAGE 2

15. What did the pelican steal? The game.

16. Who says, "You're not a postal worker, are you?" Store clerk who sells Van Pelt a gun.

17. How does Peter save the game from the river? Hangs upside down and catches it in the river.

18. What did "A law of Jumanji having been broken, you will sit back even more than your token" mean? Peter tried to drop the dice so they'd land on twelve.

19. Why does Peter begin to change to a monkey? Peter cheated.

20. Who was Carl Bentley twenty-six years ago? Stamping line at Parish Shoes.

21. How does the hunter get paint on his clothes? Alan drives into a wall of paint.

22. What causes the aunt to wreck her car? A monkey gets in her car.

23. Why does Alan tear Peter's pants? To let his tail out.

24. How does Carl finally lose his car? A vine crushes it.

25. What animal appears during the monsoon? Crocodile.

26. Whose turn ends the game? Alan.

27. What do Sarah and Alan do with the game? Throw it in the river.

28. How does the "game" continue to be alive? Some more people in another land find it.

Discussion questions: Answer these questions after the movie. Use complete sentences.

1. What does this movie seem to say about events which happen on a continuum in time? Do you agree or disagree with this theory?

2. Do you think *Jumanji* is suitable viewing for young children? Explain.

3. Describe three of the curses which occurred during the game.

4. Explain the "hook" resolution of *Jumanji*.

Name _____

HOOK RESOLUION STORIES

You will be writing a short story with a partner. Each person is to begin a story. You will write the basic situation and begin the rising action. But you will stop short of the climax.

Now trade papers with another student. You will finish the other person's story. You will write the climax and resolution, but the resolution must have some kind of "hook."

You may change any part of the original story that you like in order to have a good story. You may include dialogue, as well.

The story must be written in good form—use correct spelling, word usage, grammar, punctuation, etc.

The story must be at least 2-3 pages if it is handwritten. You may type the story if you like, but be sure to double-space and use a 12-point font. You will read your story aloud to the class.

HOOK RESOLUTION STORY RUBRIC

ELEMENTS	**W**eak (4 pts.)	**A**verage (6 pts.)	**G**ood (8 pts.)	**E**xcellent (10 pts.)
Basic Situation Characters Introduced				
Setting Introduced				
Conflict Introduced				
Conflict developed				
Climax				
Resolution With hook				
Effort/neatness				
Sentence Structure (no fragments or run-ons)				

Spelling (10 points, five points off for each error)_____

Grammar, punctuation, word choice, other (10 points)_____   Total Points: ____/100

chapter 3
An Unforgettable Character

Anne of Green Gables:
Characterization Methods

OBJECTIVES

- Students will be able to define indirect and direct characterization.
- Students will practice public speaking skills and listening skills.
- Students will learn to write and punctuate dialogue correctly.
- Students will write a character sketch using characterization techniques.

NOTES TO THE TEACHER

Anne of Green Gables (1985 TV version directed by Kevin Sullivan) is a story about Anne Shirley, an orphan who is raised by Marilla and her brother Matthew. Anne gets into trouble in spite of her efforts to be good. The story, which takes place in Canada, covers several years. This "coming of age" story is rich in characterization.

*Anne of Green Gable*s is rated G and is 199 minutes long.

POSSIBLE PROBLEMS

None.

PROCEDURES:

1. **Free Write**—Students write for ten minutes on the following topic: A person who scared me. Or place a picture on the overhead and have students write about the person.

2. **Characterization Methods**—Use the teacher activity sheet to get students to perform skits and then list characterization methods.

3. **Character Sketch from Great expectations**—Students read the excerpt and then answer the discussion questions which follow.

4. ***Anne of Green Gables* Background Information**—Go to this web address to access information to share with your students about this movie: <http://www.gov.pe.ca/infopei/index.php3?number=81411>

5. ***Anne of Green Gables* Viewing Guide**—Students answer the questions as they watch the movie.

6. **Driver's Permit Day**—Use this handout to show students how to punctuate a dialogue properly.

7. **Dialogue Writing Exercise**—Use this exercise to get students to write and punctuate original dialogues correctly and then read them aloud to the class.

8. **How to Write a Character Sketch**—Use this handout to show students how to plan a character sketch.

9. **Character Sketch Example and Assignment**—Use this handout to get students to write character sketches about one of the characters from *Anne of Green Gables*.

10. **Character Sketch Rubric**—Use this rubric to assign grades to students' writing.

CHARACTERIZATION METHODS

1. Make photocopies of these situations and cut into four strips. Choose four groups of three students and have them perform the situations as impromptu skits.
2. Have the class choose one of the skits to analyze. Make a list on the board for each character in the skit. List adjectives to describe each character.
3. Ask the students to tell you how they knew this person was disloyal, or how they knew this person was cocky, etc.
4. Now construct a list of indirect characterization methods.
5. Now define direct characterization.

Indirect Characterization

The audience/reader makes judgments about a character's personality based on the following:

1. The character's appearance
2. The character's speech
3. The character's actions
4. What other characters say about him

Direct Characterization

The author tells the audience/reader directly what the character is like. Novel and short story writers use direct characterization.

Normally scripts must rely on indirect characterization. We must watch the characters interact and form opinions about them.

In movies, the direct characterization is done through what is called a "voice over"; a narrator's voice gives details of the story.

Skit Ideas for Improvisations:

Two students are talking about the beauty pageant held at the high school over the weekend. They are talking about the winner when she walks in.

A boy is talking to another boy about his "blind" date over the weekend. Then the girl walks in.

Two teachers are talking about a student who causes trouble. Then the student walks up.

Two people are discussing their friend who has bad breath. Then the friend walks up.

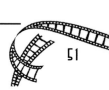

Name _____

Character Sketch from Great Expectations

Chapter 2

My sister, Mrs. Joe Gargery, was more than twenty years older than I, and had established a great reputation with herself and the neighbours because she had brought me up "by hand." Having at that time to find out for myself what the expression meant, and knowing her to have a hard and heavy hand, and to be much in the habit of laying it upon her husband as well as upon me, I supposed that Joe Gargery and I were both brought up by hand.

She was not a good-looking woman, my sister; and I had a general impression that she must have made Joe Gargery marry her by hand. Joe was a fair man, with curls of flaxen hair on each side of his smooth face, and with eyes of such a very undecided blue that they seemed to have somehow got mixed with their own whites. He was a mild, good-natured, sweet-tempered, easy-going, foolish, dear fellow - a sort of Hercules in strength, and also in weakness.

My sister, Mrs. Joe, with black hair and eyes, had such a prevailing redness of skin that I sometimes used to wonder whether it was possible she washed herself with a nutmeg-grater instead of soap. She was tall and bony, and almost always wore a coarse apron, fastened over her figure behind with two loops, and having a square impregnable bib in front, that was stuck full of pins and needles. She made it a powerful merit in herself, and a strong reproach against Joe, that she wore this apron so much. Though I really see no reason why she should have worn it at all: or why, if she did wear it at all, she should not have taken it off, every day of her life.

Great Expectations Discussion Questions

Answer these questions about the excerpt in complete sentences:

1. What does Mrs. Joe Gargery look like? Give specific detail mentioned.

2. What are some of the actions she does which show her personality?

3. What do other characters say about her—especially her brother Pip who is narrating the story?

4. What do you think her speech would be like? Construct two lines of dialogue which might show the way she would talk.

Name _____

ANNE OF GREEN GABLES VIEWING GUIDE

Briefly identify these characters as you watch the movie:

1. Megan Follows .... Anne Shirley—

2. Colleen Dewhurst .... Marilla Cuthbert—

3. Richard Farnsworth .... Matthew Cuthbert—

4. Patricia Hamilton .... Rachel Lynde—

5. Marilyn Lightstone .... Miss Stacy—

6. Schuyler Grant .... Diana Barry—

7. Jonathan Crombie .... Gilbert Blythe—

8. Charmion King .... Aunt Josephine—

9. Jackie Burroughs .... Mrs. Amelia Evans—

10. Rosemary Radcliffe .... Mrs. Barry—

Answer these questions as you watch the movie:

1. What book is Anne reading as the movie opens?

2. How does Mr. Hammond die?

3. What happened to Anne's parents?

4. Why do Matthew and Marilla want an orphan boy?

5. Why doesn't Matthew tell Anne that he wanted a boy?

6. Why can't Anne be perfectly happy?

7. How does Marilla define "dispair"?

8. Why does Marilla decide to keep Anne?

9. What is the main reason Anne doesn't want to go with Mrs. Blewett?

10. What two things does Anne pray for?

11. What is humorous about Anne's first attempt to pray?

 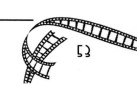

ANNE OF GREEN GABLES VIEWING GUIDE PAGE 2

12. Why does Anne shout at Rachel Lynde when they first meet?

13. How does Matthew convince Anne to apologize to Rachel Lynde?

14. Describe how Anne tricks Mrs. Lynde with her "apology."

15. Who is Katie Moore?

16. Why won't Marilla let Anne call her Aunt Marilla?

17. Why doesn't Anne like the dresses Marilla has selected for her?

18. What does Anne admit to doing when Marilla asked her about the amethyst brooch?

19. What does Marilla tell Matthew she thinks happened to the brooch?

20. Why does Anne make a false confession?

21. What actually happened to the brooch?

22. Why does Anne break her tablet over Gilbert's head?

23. Why does Marilla cut Anne's hair?

24. What does Diana say happened in Marilla's love life?

25. Why must Anne sit next to Gilbert Blithe?

26. Who wins the spelling bee?

27. How does Anne sprain her ankle?

28. What does Diana drink instead of Raspberry Cordial during her visit?

29. Why must Anne and Diana be "secret" friends?

30. Describe Miss Stacey's teaching methods.

31. What does Anne find in the pudding sauce?

32. When does Anne confess about the mouse?

23. Why didn't Matthew ever court a girl?

34. Why does Mrs. Barry forgive Anne for intoxicating Diana?

35. How does Matthew convince Marilla to let Anne go to the ball?

REEL WRITING

ANNE OF GREEN GABLES VIEWING GUIDE PAGE 3

36. What does Matthew buy for Anne when he buys the rake and brown sugar?

37. How do the girls meet Aunt Josephine?

38. Why does Aunt Josephine reinstate Diana's music lessons?

39. Where does Aunt Josephine take Anne and Diana after Anne's test?

40. Who rescues Anne from the lake?

41. What were the results of the Queens' test?

42. Why won't Anne go to the White Sands concert with Gilbert?

43. Why does Anne consider herself rich?

44. What award does Anne win?

45. What award does Gilbert win?

46. Who asks permission to date Gilbert?

47. Who was Marilla's beau?

48. Where is Anne going to teach?

ANNE OF GREEN GABLES VIEWING GUIDE—TEACHER

1. What book is Anne reading as the movie opens? Camelot.

2. How does Mr. Hammond die? Heart attack.

3. What happened to Anne's parents? Died of the fever when she was three.

4. Why do Matthew and Marilla want an orphan boy? Help with the chores.

5. Why doesn't Matthew tell Anne that he wanted a boy? He doesn't want to hurt her feelings. He likes her.

6. Why can't Anne be perfectly happy? She has red hair.

7. How does Marilla define "despair"? Turning your back on God.

8. Why does Marilla decide to keep Anne? She dislikes Mrs. Blewett.

9. What is the main reason Anne doesn't want to go with Mrs. Blewett? Mrs. Blewett has two sets of twins.

10. What two things does Anne pray for? Stay at Green Gables and to be beautiful.

11. What is humorous about Anne's first attempt to pray? She closes it like a letter.

12. Why does Anne shout at Rachel Lynde when they meet? Rachel said she was skinny and had carrot red hair.

13. How does Matthew convince Anne to apologize to Rachel Lynde? She doesn't have to really mean it and he wants her to.

14. Describe how Anne tricks Mrs. Lynde with her "apology." Says she shouldn't have said she was mean even if it was true.

15. Who is Katie Moore? The girl in Anne's reflection.

16. Why won't Marilla let Anne call her Aunt Marilla? She's not Anne's aunt.

17. Why doesn't Anne like the dresses Marilla has selected for her? They don't have puffed sleeves.

18. What does Anne admit to doing when Marilla asked her about the amethyst brooch? She tried it on.

19. What does Marilla tell Matthew she thinks happened to the brooch? Anne stole it.

20. Why does Anne make a false confession? So she can go to the picnic.

21. What actually happened to the brooch? It was caught on Marilla's shall.

22. Why does Anne break her tablet over Gilbert's head? He called her carrot and pulled her hair.

23. Why does Marilla cut Anne's hair? Anne dyed it green.

24. What does Diana say happened in Marilla's love life? Quarreled with her beau and refused to forgive him.

REEL WRITING

ANNE OF GREEN GABLES VIEWING GUIDE—TEACHER PAGE 2

25. Why must Anne sit next to Gilbert Blithe? She fought with them to avenge Diana.

26. Who wins the spelling bee? Anne.

27. How does Anne sprain her ankle? Falls off a roof and in a well.

28. What does Diana drink instead of Raspberry Cordial during her visit? Wine.

29. Why must Anne and Diana be "secret" friends? Diana's mother forbids their friendship.

30. Describe Miss Stacey's teaching methods. Field trips, hands on.

31. What does Anne find in the pudding sauce? Mouse.

32. When does Anne confess about the mouse? As Miss Stacey is about to eat the pudding.

33. Why didn't Matthew ever court a girl? He would have to talk to her.

34. Why does Mrs. Barry forgive Anne for intoxicating Diana? Anne saved the baby from the croup.

35. How does Matthew convince Marilla to let Anne go to the ball? Said Marilla never went to a ball.

36. What does Matthew buy for Anne when he buys the rake and brown sugar? Dress with puffy sleeves.

37. How do the girls meet Aunt Josephine? Jump in bed with her.

38. Why does Aunt Josephine reinstate Diana's music lessons? Says the girls must come to visit her.

39. Where does Aunt Josephine take Anne and Diana after Anne's test? Opera.

40. Who rescues Anne from the lake when she pretends to be the Lady of Chalotte? Gilbert.

41. What were the results of the Queens' test? Anne and Gilbert tie for top score.

42. Why won't Anne go to the White Sands concert with Gilbert? She thinks it will displease Marilla.

43. Why does Anne consider herself rich? She has sixteen years and an imagination.

44. What award does Anne win from the college? Scholarship.

45. What award does Gilbert win at college? Gold medal.

46. Who asks Anne for permission to date Gilbert? Diana.

47. Who was Marilla's beau when she was younger? Gilbert's father.

48. Where is Anne going to teach? Avonlea School.

DRIVER'S PERMIT DAY
by Karla Hardaway

"Number eighty!" Michael and I approached the counter. I put down the paper number. "What are you doing here?" a middle-aged woman with wild hair barked as she waved our number.

"You called number eighty?"

"No, I didn't!" She looked around us and called, "Seventy-nine!" No one came. After a minute, she sighed and rolled her eyes. "All right. Come here!"

"We're here to get his driving permit," I explained.

"Do you have his birth certificate, driver's education form, and proof of insurance?"

"No, we brought his military ID card."

"You have to have a birth certificate." Her eyes got larger.

"A few weeks ago, I brought his twin sister in, and the clerk wouldn't take the birth certificate because it was just notarized and not original. But she accepted Shannon's ID card."

"Who did that?" she screamed. "They're not supposed to do that! I need to know who it was so I can find out why they broke the rules. That's against policy!"

I pointed to the cubical I remembered.

"Well, is that her?"

"I don't remember."

"You don't remember? Was she white or black?"

"I don't remember."

"You don't remember?" Her voice dripped vinegar.

"If I say it was her, I'd be lying, because I don't remember."

The woman grabbed our papers and disappeared through a door in the back. A few minutes later she returned. "I got permission to accept his ID card. It's against the rules, but my boss said to do it."

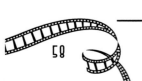

DRIVER'S PERMIT DAY
PAGE 2

"I really appreciate it."

"Well, don't appreciate me too much because I wouldn't have done it. I like my job too much."

I couldn't help rolling my eyes. "Okay then, I don't appreciate it." She clenched her teeth and continued writing. Michael shot me a look warning me not to mess things up.

Then she barked to Michael, "Look through the lens and read the first three lines!"

Then I remembered Michael's poor eyesight. He needed glasses but refused to wear them. He peered into the machine and said, "2-4-6-3-3-8-9. 0-9-5-5-7-2-1. 9-6-7-2-2-8." He smiled and backed away.

"Absolutely not!" the woman screamed. "Try the third line again!"

Michael looked into the machine again. He took his time. I could tell he was trying to blur his eye so he could read the numbers. "9-6-8-0-0-9."

"Good." Our first positive response. She gave him his test and instructed him where to sit. While He was taking his test, I sat and fumed. I couldn't believe I had allowed an adult to treat my child so rudely. She had all the power. If we wanted his driving permit, we had to subject ourselves to her rudeness. I decided that a requirement for working at the driver's license bureau must be rudeness and a quest for power.

Michael finished his test and handed it to her to be graded.

"That didn't take you very long," she said.

"He's very smart, " I answered.

As she went row by row with no missed answers, she began to soften. "Yes, he is very smart. He only missed two. That's very good." She smiled. "Sign here, and congratulations." Now she was all nice. We paid the eighteen dollars, got his picture made, and left.

As soon as we were through the doors, we both dissolved into laughter. "I'm sorry I let her be so rude to you."

He just stared at his permit and said, "I'm just glad I passed the eye test. That was awesome. She let me take it twice." Michael was in shock. He didn't even ask me if he could drive home.

DIALOGUE WRITING EXERCISE

Divide the class into pairs. One student in each pair should write an opening line of dialogue on the page. The line should hint at the personality and age of the person who is saying it. Example: "How many times do I have to tell you to clean up your room?"

The paper then passes to the partner. He reads the line and then decides what kind of character would respond. He then writes a line of dialogue in response.

Students continue to exchange the paper adding lines of dialogue to create a conversation. The conversation should include at least fifteen lines of dialogue punctuated correctly. Tell students to be sure to indent and begin a new paragraph each time the speaker changes and to be sure to put quotes around the words spoken aloud and to separate lines of dialogue from dialogue tags (the "he said" part).

When students are finished, each pair goes to the front of the class to read their dialogues aloud. The students then explain who they envisioned each character to be. The amazing part is that the dialogue helps to define the characters. This is a good exercise to show indirect characterization through what the character says and what others say about him.

Name _____

HOW TO WRITE A CHARACTER SKETCH

A character sketch is a written "portrait" of a person. The skills you learn in writing character sketches can be used in many writing situations—essay questions, persuasive essays, creative fiction, vignettes, and memoirs, for example.

When you begin to write a character sketch of a "target" person, the best place to start is to decide what kind of personality that person has. Is the person nice or mean? A good guy or a bad guy? Friendly or standoffish? Here is a list of some personality types:

mean and nasty	protective	generous	a leader
friendly	lucky	stingy	a follower
gentle	unlucky	moody	optimistic
honest	successful	crazy	pessimistic
kind	hardworking	saintly	dishonest
loving	lazy	ambitious	hateful

After you've figured out what type of personality the target person has, begin listing all of the physical characteristics of the person. Not just short or tall, fat or thin, old or young, but also try to list characteristics of the way the person dresses, moves, gestures, carries himself, and changes expression. Really observe the target closely—do you see any nervous habits, fake mannerisms, repeated gestures? Go over your list and select only those physical characteristics that help prove the personality of the character.

Then try to remember things the target has said and done. What actions or deeds has he performed in his relationships with others? How does he treat people? What decisions is he responsible for? Make a list of the deeds that will prove your portrait.

Now you select a *persona*—a voice from which to observe the target. What kind of person should you be as the observer? Can you use your own voice, or would it be more convincing to pretend to be someone else? This is important, because different observers will notice different things about the same target. (Think how differently a character sketch of you written by your mother would be from one written by your lab partner) Go over both lists you have written and make sure that each observation on each list is in keeping with the persona of the observer.

Your final step is to blend the observations of looks and deeds to convince your audience that the target is a particular personality type. Start with a strong opening sentence that defines your position. Example: "John Smith's meanness can be seen in both his appearance and his actions." Take it from there, and carefully choose each specific detail from your list to prove your point.

Here's the procedure abbreviated:
1. Make a personality statement. _____ is _____.
                              (target's name)   (personality type)
2. List all physical characteristics and mannerisms that prove your point.
3. List all deeds and actions that prove your point.
4. Choose a persona or voice to write from. Omit both looks and deeds that are out of character for the observer.
5. Write the character sketch. Begin with a clear topic sentence and blend items from both of your lists to prove your point.

CHARACTER SKETCH EXAMPLE AND ASSIGNMENT

This sheet gives an example of the five steps in writing a character sketch. Here a student went through the listing process and chose an interesting persona from which to write.

Personality statement: _____Mary_____ is __a hot head.____
                        (target's name)   (personality type)

List of physical characteristics and mannerisms, freely brainstormed:

blonde hair	*chews gum in class*
piercing blue eyes	*wears lime green shoes*
talks with hands	perfect teeth
straight A student	makes honor roll
best basketball player in gym class	

List of all deeds and actions, freely brainstormed:

volunteers to go first in class
rides home with brother
over reacts to things
always raises hand in class
tried to rip her blouse off sister
wrote friends notes in drivers education
tardy to first period
can't drive yet
hit her best friend over a boy
exaggerates stories
stomped upstairs and turned up music
slammed door

Persona: Sarah Smith: sister of Mary Smith. Italics are details Sarah wouldn't necessarily know.

CHARACTER SKETCH OF MARY SMITH

My sister Mary is a hot head. She has a tendency to over-react to things. She has always been something of a drama queen. When she tells a story, I always know that much of it is exaggerated, for effect, of course. And she sure knows how to use body language. She can take a minor incident and blow it way out of proportion. Once I borrowed her favorite blouse when she wasn't home. She was waiting at the door when I got home and almost ripped it off me. If my mom hadn't intervened when she heard the noise, I don't know what might have happened.

Mary has a hard time keeping friends. She is very pretty with piercing blue eyes, long blonde hair, and a great figure. But girls tend to be leery of her. I think people get tired of trying to figure out how to act around her. She is very friendly one day and icy the next, and she thinks all boys belong to her. She actually punched her best friend in the hall one day at school when she found out they liked the same boy. Then Mary ignored the boy when he called her to ask about the fight.

When I told her we had to clean up the house before Mom got home, she got really angry. The whites of her eyes seemed to expand rapidly as her pupils turned into little dark bulls-eyes. She screamed that I owed her a favor and should do all the cleaning. I knew I should be quiet, but I yelled back saying I wasn't her slave. Her face reddened and her breathing became short. She said she wasn't going to do a thing and she'd deal with Mom when she got home. She stomped up the stairs and went into her room. She turned her radio up as high as the speakers would go and slammed her door.

(by Sarah Smith, Mary's sister)

Assignment:
Now you are to write a character sketch for one of the characters in the movie *Anne of Green Gables*. Your persona should be another character from the movie. For example, Diana Berry might be talking about Gilbert Blythe or Marilla might be talking about Anne.

Your character sketch should be at least three well-developed paragraphs. It should be typed neatly in a 12-point font. Use correct grammar, word choice, and spelling. Etc.

You should make the brainstorm lists shown in the sample exercises. Identify the persona and the person to be characterized. Then begin the character sketch.

Example: Diana Berry writing about Gilbert Blythe.

 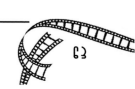

CHARACTER SKETCH RUBRIC

ELEMENTS	**W**eak (4 pts.)	**A**verage (6 pts.)	**G**ood (8 pts.)	**E**xcellent (10 pts.)
Appearance neat and typed correctly				
Physical Characteristics given				
Actions Described				
First Paragraph				
Second Paragraph				
Third Paragraph				
Brainstorm List included				

Spelling (10 points, five points off for each error)_____

Grammar, punctuation, word choice, other (10 points)_____

Total Points: _____/90

Chapter 4

Circle of Love

Places in the Heart: Symbolism

OBJECTIVES

- Students will be able to identify symbolism in literature and movies.
- Students will write a five paragraph persuasive essay.
- Students will gain editing practice by doing peer critiques of essays.

NOTES TO THE TEACHER

Places in the Heart takes place in Waxahachie, Texas, during the 1930's. Frank Spalding, the sheriff, is accidentally shot by a drunk African American boy. Several members of the town hang the young man.

Edna Spalding must find a way to keep her family together and earn a living. Moses shows up at her farm and works for her in exchange for food. She also lets a blind man board with her to get extra money.

Places in the Heart is rated PG and is 112 minutes long.

POSSIBLE PROBLEMS

Be sure to preview this movie ahead of time. Talk to the students about prejudice in the South during pre-civil rights time. There is a scene in which the Klu Klux Klan beats up Moses. Also the "n" word is used once. Be sure to tell the students that the prejudice shown and the dialect used is a reflection of the times.

The movie is well worth viewing. The focus is on brotherly love and forgiveness.

PROCEDURES

1. **Free Write**—Students write for ten minutes on the following topic to introduce *Places in the Heart*: What color is success?

2. **Brainstorming Exercise**—The teacher lists colors on the board (white, black, red, yellow, blue, purple, green, etc.). Students divided into groups decide what each color stands for.

3. **Object Symbolism**—Students retrieve objects from their purses or backpacks and brainstorm in groups what each object might represent.

4. **Symbolism Definition**—The teacher supplies the following definition to students: Symbolism is the technique of using an object or idea to stand for a larger, abstract idea.

5. **The Tiger**—Distribute copies and ask students to determine what the tiger stands for.

6. *Places in the Heart* **Viewing Guide**—Students answer these questions as they watch the movie.

7. **Steps in Writing the Five Paragraph Essay**—Distribute copies for students to use.

8. **Introduction Techniques**—Show transparency and have students copy information.

9. *Places in the Heart* **Essay**—Students will write a five paragraph essay using the following sentence as their thesis statement: Although many characters are not present by the end of the movie, each occupies a place in the heart of Edna Spalding.

10. **Student Critique Sheet**—Distribute copies and let students critique their essays. Students then rewrite their essays to turn in for a grade.

11. **Essay Rubric**—Use this rubric to assign grades to the students' essays.

THE TIGER
by Steve Hardaway

I let the tiger out of the cage. Before you say anything, I know it was a stupid thing to do. But have you ever touched a tiger?

I've always lived a very careful and conservative life, and I would never have done anything dangerous. But, maybe that's what has been wrong all along. So, when I got this chance, I just couldn't pass it up. I watched him pace back and forth for a long time. His movement was hypnotic. When I finally decided to take the risk, I carefully unlocked the door and opened it wide. I knew there were no guarantees of safety, but I just couldn't help myself. He stopped and stared at me with large, green eyes. I knew he could see right through me, and that all my soul and secrets would be his for the taking. At that moment, I knew my life would never be the same.

He exited the cage and circled me sniffing and inspecting me from head to toe. I felt some fear, but not as much as I thought I would. We were both tentative at first. I risked placing my hand on his back. He took notice but didn't seem to mind. At one point he turned to face me, barred his fangs, and roared. But he didn't attack, and our uneasy relationship continued to grow.

Over time we became closer and I was able to pet him. His fur was incredibly soft. I thought my fingertips would melt right into it. The colors were vivid and crisp, and the smell of this great beast was burned into my mind forever. But just under that stimulating exterior, I could see and feel the powerful muscles. His razor-sharp claws were safely retracted into their sheaths, but I knew they were there. And I knew what they could do.

At one point, he became playful. He bounced around in front of me, and I tried to grab one of his ears. This huge, wild animal frolicked like a kitten without a trace of malice in his mind. He seemed intent only on having fun, and for a moment I forgot about his true nature. Touching and playing with him is the most dangerous and the most wonderful experience of my life.

I'm sitting very still now, and he is lying beside me with his gigantic head in my lap. Heavy breathing seems to indicate he's taking a nap, but I can never be sure. I trace gentle circles on his head with my finger, hoping that the caressing will keep him pacified. His huge body and awesome power are overwhelmingly beautiful, but one of his long claws pokes my leg as a gentle reminder of what he is capable of doing.

So, should I put the tiger back into the cage? There is nothing to keep him from attacking and ripping me into shreds, and if he turns on me, I won't last ten seconds. I seem to have control right now, and I believe my ability to judge and control him is increasing over time, but am I getting overly confident? I've seen clips on television of wild animals turning on their trainers; in some ways it seems so inevitable, so natural. The victim's face always shows a look of surprise. But look at him, touch him. He's magnificent! I feed on his power, and it makes my life worth living. I keep thinking I should put the tiger back in the cage, but I just can't.

What do you think the tiger symbolizes? Quote at least five lines from the text to support your answers and explain each.

Name _____

PLACES IN THE HEART VIEWING GUIDE

Briefly identify these characters as you watch the movie:

1. Sally Field .... Edna Spalding—

2. Lindsay Crouse .... Margaret Lomax—

3. Ed Harris .... Wayne Lomax—

4. Amy Madigan .... Viola Kelsey—

5. John Mallcovich .... Mr. Will—

6. Danny Glover .... Moses/Moze—

7. Yankton Hatten .... Frank Spalding—

8. Gennie Hames .... Possum Spalding—

Sally Field won an Oscar for Best Actress in a Leading Role in 1984.
Robert Benton won an Oscar for Best Writing of a Screenplay in 1984.

Answer these questions as you watch the movie:

1. List the opening shots in the film (that accompany the credits). What mood is established by them?

2. When and where does the movie open?

3. What do you think is the purpose of the scene in the Spalding dining room at Sunday dinner?

4. Why is the sheriff called away during his dinner?

5. How does the sheriff get killed?

6. What happens to Wiley?

7. Where do Wayne and Viola meet to have an affair?

8. What one building in town dominates as the key visual image throughout the film? Why?

9. What is the first interaction between Edna and Moses?

10. What does Moses offer to do for Edna in exchange for a place to stay?

Name _____

PLACES IN THE HEART VIEWING GUIDE PAGE 2

11. Why does Edna save Moses when the officer catches him with her silver?

12. Why does Edna take in Mr. Will as a border?

13. What traits make up Edna's character? What values seem to guide her life?

14. How is Edna's grief expressed in the film? Give two occasions.

15. How does the tornado make Edna, her children, Moses, and Mr. Will into a family?

16. What does the tornado represent to Viola and Wayne?

17. How does Edna plan to earn an extra $100 to save her farm?

18. How does Margaret realize Viola and Wayne are involved in an affair? How does she react?

19. How does Mr. Will help in the cotton picking?

20. How does Edna describe herself to Mr. Will?

21. How does Mr. Will try to save Moses from the Klan?

22. After Moses is beat up by the Ku Klux Klan members, why is he crying?

23. When Edna says goodbye to Moses, what three gifts does he give her?

24. What gift does Edna give to Moses?

Discussion questions: Answer these questions in complete sentences after you watch the movie.

1. In what ways do Edna's relationships with Moses and Mr. Will represent the theme of brotherly love in the movie?

2. Describe the communion scene in the church. List the people who are present. What do you think the symbolism of the scene is?

Name _____

PLACES IN THE HEART VIEWING GUIDE—TEACHER

Briefly identify these characters as you watch the movie:

1. Sally Field .... Edna Spalding—

2. Lindsay Crouse .... Margaret Lomax—

3. Ed Harris .... Wayne Lomax—

4. Amy Madigan .... Viola Kelsey—

5. John Mallcovich .... Mr. Will—

6. Danny Glover .... Moses/Moze—

7. Yankton Hatten .... Frank Spalding—

8. Gennie Hames .... Possum Spalding—

   Sally Field won an Oscar for Best Actress in a Leading Role in 1984.
   Robert Benton won an Oscar for Best Writing of a Screenplay in 1984.

Answer these questions as you watch the movie:

1. List the opening shots in the film (that accompany the credits). What mood is established by them? Churches, a family in a restaurant, a car with homeless people, farmhouse, dirt road, a man begging, train, a white family praying over a meal, purple flowers, a black family praying over a meal, windmill, farmhouse. It feely homey, safe.

2. When and where does the movie open? Waxahachie, Texas, 1935.

3. What do you think is the purpose of the scene in the Spalding dining room at Sunday dinner? Family dependent on the father.

4. Why is the sheriff called away during his dinner? Wiley is drunk and shooting a gun.

5. How does the sheriff get killed? Wiley accidentally shoots him. Wiley thought the bullets were gone.

6. What happens to Wiley? Gets dragged by a truck and hanged.

7. Where do Wayne and Viola meet to have an affair? Deserted house.

8. What one building in town dominates as the key visual image throughout the film? Why? Church. Stands for brotherly love and forgiveness.

9. What is the first interaction between Edna and Moses? She gives him a plate of food.

Name _____

PLACES IN THE HEART VIEWING GUIDE—TEACHER PAGE 2

10. What does Moses offer to do for Edna in exchange for a place to stay? Chores. Plant cotton,

11. Why does Edna save Moses when the officer catches him with her silver? She needs him to plant cotton to save her farm.

12. Why does Edna take in Mr. Will as a border? Get money for mortgage.

13. What traits make up Edna's character? What values seem to guide her life? Determined. She loves her children. She's not afraid of hard work.

14. How is Edna's grief expressed in the film? Give two occasions. She has to whip Frank and she dreams about dancing with her husband.

15. How does the tornado make Edna, her children, Moses, and Mr. Will into a family? They help each other.

16. What does the tornado represent to Viola and Wayne? The end of their affair.

17. How does Edna plan to earn an extra $100 to save her farm? Get the first bale of cotton in.

18. How does Margaret realize Viola and Wayne are involved in an affair? How does she react? Sees them talking in the bedroom when they play cards. Lots of weird looks at the table. She kicks Wayne out.

19. How does Mr. Will help in the cotton picking? He cooks.

20. How does Edna describe herself to Mr. Will? Long hair, brown eyes, teeth stick out, no real beauty.

21. How does Mr. Will try to save Moses from the Klan? Shoots a gun.

22. After Moses is beat up by the Ku Klux Klan members, why is he crying? He knows he must leave to protect Edna and her children.

23. When Edna says goodbye to Moses, what three gifts does he give her? Horseshoe, handkerchief, doll.

24. What gift does Edna give to Moses? Respect for a job well done.

Discussion questions: Answer these questions in complete sentences after you watch the movie.

1. In what ways do Edna's relationships with Moses and Mr. Will represent the theme of brotherly love in the movie?

2. Describe the communion scene in the church. List the people who are present. What do you think the symbolism of the scene is?

STEPS IN WRITING THE FIVE PARAGRAPH ESSAY

I. Thesis statement—A thesis statement is the *core* of any essay. It should state very simply what will be *proven* in the essay. Therefore, it must be *debatable* or contain *ambiguous* words which must be defined. A student should take the general topic a teacher supplies him, consider how he *feels* about it, and then convert it to an opinion statement.

Examples:

Topic	Thesis
1. dogs	Dogs are smarter than cats.
	Dogs are more affectionate than cats.
	Cats are smarter than dogs.
2. school	A student should be able to pass an exit exam before receiving a high school diploma.
	Many parents consider school a free babysitting service.
	A high school drop-out may be smarter than the public believes he is.
	The school is beginning adopt the role of teaching values to our youth.
3. television	People love violence in television programs.
	The "soap opera" allows housewives to escape their own problems.
	The media determines public opinion.
4. death	Everyone believes in some type of life-after-death.
	No one can adequately prepare himself for death.
	When a person dies, his survivors mourn out of selfishness.

II. After the thesis statement is determined, the next step is to prove the statement. At least three proofs should follow a good thesis sentence.

Examples:
1. Dogs are smarter than cats.
   A. Dogs learn tricks, but cats do not.
   B. Dogs are used in circus acts.
   C. Dogs are trained by the military for protection and to find drugs.
   D. Dogs are used as seeing-eye dogs for the blind.

2. People love violence in television programs.
   A. Many television movies deal with real life murder stories.
   B. News stories dealing with violence, complete with pictures, receive top priority on network news programs.
   C. Police shows amass large audiences.

III. The next step in writing an essay is to expand each proof into a paragraph using details and explanations. Each proof sentence becomes the topic sentence of a paragraph.

IV. The thesis statement appears two times in the essay—at the end of the first paragraph, the introduction, and at the beginning of the last paragraph, the conclusion. It should be restated in the conclusion, but should echo the original thesis statement.

Name _____

STEPS IN WRITING THE FIVE PARAGRAPH ESSAY PAGE 2

V. The conclusion is just a summary of what the essay has already said. It should restate the thesis in different words and then summarize the main ideas from each body paragraph. The author may also give his own opinion in the conclusion, or he may offer solutions to a problem which he has introduced in his essay.

A writer should never begin a conclusion with the words "In conclusion." It should be obvious that the conclusion is starting.

The conclusion should end with a clincher sentence which makes the essay sound finished.

INTRODUCTION

The following methods may be used in writing an introduction for an essay:

1. Rhetorical question—Ask a question or several questions which challenge the reader to think about the topic.

2. State an unusual fact or statistic.

3. Refer to a historical event.

4. Point to common relationships, interests, or opinions.

5. Refer to occasion.

6. Present a quotation.

7. Anecdote—Tell a true or fictional story related to the topic.

8. Mystery—Begin with a series of clues which gradually reveal more and more about your topic.

Name _____

STUDENT CRITIQUE SHEET

Name of person's essay which you are critiquing _____

1. Is the essay double-spaced using a 12 point font?

2. How does the introduction get your attention? Are there at least four or five sentences?

3. What is the thesis? Is it clear? Offer revision ideas if it is not.

4. What is the topic sentence of the first body paragraph? Does it support the thesis? Offer revisions if it does not. Is the paragraph developed enough? Explain.

5. What is the topic sentence of the second body paragraph? Does it support the thesis? Offer revisions if it does not. Is the paragraph developed enough? Explain.

6. What is the topic sentence of the third body paragraph? Does it support the thesis? Offer revisions if it does not. Is the paragraph developed enough? Explain.

7. Does the conclusion start with a rewritten statement of the thesis? Write it down. Does the conclusion summarize the main points of the essay and end with a clincher sentence? Offer suggestions for revision if it does not.

Name _____

ESSAY EVALUATION RUBRIC

	Weak (4 pts.)	Average (6 pts.)	Good (8 pts.)	Excellent (10 pts.)
Appearance				
Introduction (development and strategy)				
Clear Thesis				
Body I (Topic sentence, developed)				
Body II (Topic sentence, developed)				
Body III (Topic sentence, developed)				
Conclusion (Thesis, summary, clincher)				
Sentence structure (Run-ons, fragments)				

Spelling (10 points, five points off for each error)_____

Grammar, punctuation, word choice, other (10 points)_____

Total Points:_____/100

OBJECTIVES

- Students will become familiar with proverbs and adages.
- Students will practice acting skills.
- Students will be able to identify the theme of a motion picture.
- Students will be able to identify puns.
- Student will learn to write a film review.

NOTES TO THE TEACHER

Miracle on 34th Street is a family favorite. Mrs. Walker has carefully taught her daughter Susan that Santa Claus is not real. But when Kris Kringle enters their lives, mother and daughter are forced to re-examine their beliefs. The movie shows the power of belief in the unknown.

Miracle on 34th Street is rated PG and is 114 minutes long.

POSSIBLE PROBLEMS

None.

PROCEDURES

1. **Charades Game with Proverbs and Adages**—Use this information to lead the class in a charades game using proverbs and adages. Then tell the students that proverb type ideas are often used as themes in literature. Copy the proverbs list and cut into strips to use in the game.

2. **Theme**—Use this transparency to give the students the definition of theme.

3. *Miracle on 34th Street* **Viewing Guide**—Students answer these questions as they watch the movie.

4. **Just for Fun—Christmas Puns**—Make a transparency from these pages. Give students the definition of a pun. Cover the transparency on the overhead with another solid sheet of paper and reveal the question. Then move the paper down one line at a time to reveal the answers.

5. **Writing a Film Review**—Students construct a film review on *Miracle on 34th Street* or any movie the teacher wants to use.

Teacher

CHARADES GAME WITH PROVERBS AND ADAGES

Divide class into teams. Each row can be a team, or possibly two rows if the class is small.

Proverbs should be cut in strips and placed in a cup from which to draw.

One member from the team draws a slip. As soon as he begins to perform, his time starts. He has up to two minutes to get the team to guess. When someone guesses correctly, the time stops. The time used becomes his points earned. The object is to get the team to guess in the shortest amount of time possible. If the team doesn't guess, the same proverb goes to the next team. Or you can start over each time, if you like.

Someone (probably the teacher) should keep a tally of time used by each team. At the end of the game, the team with the *least* points (time used to guess) wins.

Charades symbols are traditionally as follows:
Pulls on ear means "sounds like."
Holds up fingers (two, three, six, etc.) means "number of words in phrase."
Taps fingers on inside of elbow means "number of syllables in the word."

For the film class, this game is used to introduce universal themes used in literature.

PROVERBS

A bird in the hand is worth two in the bush.

A friend in need is a friend indeed.

A man is known by the company he keeps.

All work and no play make Jack a dull boy.

An apple a day keeps the doctor away.

Curiosity killed the cat.

Don't count your chickens before they're hatched.

Don't judge a book by its cover.

It's the little things in life that count.

Never swap horses in the middle of the stream.

No pain, no gain.

Old habits die hard.

The shortest distance between two points is a straight line.

Too many cooks spoil the broth.

When the cat's away, the mice will play.

Absence makes the heart grow fonder.

Actions speak louder than words.

A fool and his money are soon parted.

A little knowledge is a dangerous thing.

A penny saved is a penny earned.

A picture is worth a thousand words.

A rolling stone gathers no moss.

A stitch in time saves nine.

All good things come to an end.

All's fair in love and war.

All's well that ends well.

All that glitters is not gold.

Good things come to him who waits.

An ounce of prevention is worth a pound of cure.

April showers bring May flowers.

Ask and you shall receive.

A watched pot never boils.

A woman's work is never done.

Beauty is in the eye of the beholder.

Better late than never.

Better safe than sorry.

Blood is thicker than water.

Boys will be boys.

Don't cast your pearls before swine.

Desperate times call for desperate measures.

Different strokes for different folks.

Don't burn your bridges before they're crossed.

Don't count your chickens before they're hatched.

Don't cry over spilt milk.

Don't cut off your nose to spite your face.

Don't put all your eggs in one basket.

Don't put the cart before the horse.

Don't throw out the baby with the bathwater.

The early bird catches the worm.

Every cloud has a silver lining.

Familiarity breeds contempt.

Fool me once, shame on you. Fool me twice, shame on me.

Garbage in, garbage out.

Good fences make good neighbors.

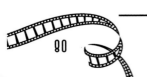

REEL WRITING

PROVERBS   PAGE 2

Haste makes waste.

Have not, want not.

His bark is worse than his bite.

History repeats itself.

Home is where the heart is.

Honesty is the best policy.

Honey catches more flies than vinegar.

If a thing is worth doing, it's worth doing well.

If the shoe fits, wear it.

If you can't beat them, join them.

If it rains, it pours.

It takes two to tango.

Kill two birds with one stone.

Let sleeping dogs lie.

Look before you leap.

Love is blind.

Misery loves company.

Don't judge a book by its cover.

Don't put off 'til tomorrow what you should do today.

No man is an island.

One good turn deserves another.

One man's trash is another man's treasure.

Out of sight, out of mind.

People who live in glass houses shouldn't throw stones.

Practice makes perfect.

Rules are made to be broken.

Still waters run deep.

Talk is cheap.

The best things in life are free.

The end justifies the means.

The grass is always greener on the other side.

The spirit is willing, but the flesh is weak.

There's more than one way to skin a cat.

Truth is stranger than fiction.

Two heads are better than one.

Two's company, three's a crowd.

Two wrongs don't make a right.

That which doesn't kill you makes you stronger.

You can't have your cake and eat it, too.

You can't teach an old dog new tricks.

You scratch my back and I'll scratch yours.

You lose some and you gain some.

That's just a drop in the bucket.

Sink or swim.

He's a little wet behind the ears.

He's like a fish out of water.

THEME

What is theme**?**

Fable—The theme of a fable is the moral it teaches.

Parable—The theme of a parable is the lesson it teaches.

Fiction—The theme of fiction does not usually teach or preach. It may not even be presented directly at all. The reader figures it out from the characters, the action, and the setting. It is implied by the story.

The theme of a story is the underlying truth it communicates.

Common Themes in Literature

Friendship

Family

Individuality

Freedom

Dealing with Death

Dealing with Loss

The American Dream

Overcoming Difficulties

Heroes

Growing Up

The Power of Believing

Generation Gap

Marriage Relationships

Maturation Journey

Life's Journey

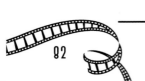

Name _____

MIRACLE ON 34TH STREET VIEWING GUIDE

Briefly identify each character as you watch the movie:

1. Richard Attenborough .... Kris Kringle/Santa Clause—

2. Elizabeth Perkins .... Dorey Walker—

3. Mara Wilson .... Susan Walker—

4. Dylan McDermott .... Bryan Bedford—

5. Robert Prosky .... Judge Henry Harper—

6. J.T. Walsh .... Ed Collins—

7. James Remar .... Mr. Jack Duff—

8. William Windom .... C.F. Cole—

Answer these questions as you watch the movie:

1. Why does Kris object to the man playing Santa Claus in the Coles Thanksgiving Day Parade?

2. Kris accepts the job as Santa under what condition?

3. From where does Susan watch the parade?

4. What secret does Susan know about Santa which she confesses to Bryan? Who teaches her?

5. Who wants to ask the blessing at the Thanksgiving dinner? Why do you think Dorey doesn't pray?

6. Why does Mr. Macy want to keep Kris Kringle as Santa even though he sends people to other stores when Coles doesn't have certain stock or the prices are too high?

7. What idea do Dorey and Ed present to Mr. Macy about product availability?

8. Why doesn't Susan ask Santa for anything?

9. Why does Dorey teach Susan that there is no Santa?

10. According to Kris Kringle's employment application, where was he born?

11. What store tries to steal Kris as Santa?

12. How does Santa visit every house around the world in one night?

Name _____

MIRACLE ON 34TH STREET VIEWING GUIDE PAGE 2

13. How does Santa begin to convince Susan that he is real?

14. How does Dorey suggest to Susan that Susan prove the reality or fantasy of Santa?

15. What does Santa claim he is a symbol for?

16. Who baby-sits for Susan when Dorey and Bryan go out?

17. What does Susan ask Santa for?

18. What present does Bryan offer to Dorey? What does she call him?

19. To whom does Bryan give the ring?

20. Why does Santa get arrested?

21. Why does the judge wait to sign Kris' commitment papers?

22. How does Coles show its support for Kris before his hearing?

23. Who is Mr. Bedford's first witness?

24. Who is Mr. Bedford's second witness?

25. Who confirms to the Collins children that Kris was the real Santa?

26. Why can't Kris make the reindeer fly?

27. How does Susan convince the Judge that Santa is real?

28. Does Susan get what she wanted from Santa for Christmas? Explain.

Discussion: Answer these questions in complete sentences after you watch the movie.

1. Do you believe parents should allow their children to believe in Santa Claus or should they tell them the truth? Explain.

2. What is the theme of *Miracle on 34th Street?* Which characters help develop the theme?

MIRACLE ON 34TH STREET VIEWING GUIDE—TEACHER

Briefly identify each character as you watch the movie:

1. Richard Attenborough .... Kris Kringle/Santa Clause—

2. Elizabeth Perkins .... Dorey Walker—

3. Mara Wilson .... Susan Walker—

4. Dylan McDermott .... Bryan Bedford—

5. Robert Prosky .... Judge Henry Harper—

6. J.T. Walsh .... Ed Collins—

7. James Remar .... Mr. Jack Duff—

8. William Windom .... C.F. Cole—

Answer these questions as you watch the movie:

1. Why does Kris object to the man playing Santa Claus in the Coles Thanksgiving Day Parade? He is drunk.

2. Kris accepts the job as Santa under what condition? He wants to use his own uniform.

3. From where does Susan watch the parade? Bryan Bedford's apartment.

4. What secret does Susan know about Santa which she confesses to Bryan? Who told her? Santa's not real. Her mom.

5. Who wants to ask the blessing at the Thanksgiving dinner? Why do you think Dorey doesn't pray? Bryan. Dorey has no faith.

6. Why does Mr. Macy want to keep Kris Kringle as Santa even though he sends people to other stores when Coles doesn't have certain stock or the prices are too high? Customers love it—Comes gains customer loyalty.

7. What idea do Dorey and Ed present to Mr. Macy about product availability? If Coles doesn't have it, we'll send you to someone who does.

8. Why doesn't Susan ask Santa for anything? She says her mom buys her presents.

9. Why does Dorey teach Susan that there is no Santa? Teaches reality, not fantasy.

10. According to Kris Kringle's employment application, where was he born? North Pole

11. What store tries to steal Kris as Santa? Shopper's Express.

MIRACLE ON 34TH STREET VIEWING GUIDE—TEACHER PAGE 2

12. How does Santa visit every house around the world in one night? He slows time down.

13. How does Santa begin to convince Susan that he is real? Speaks sign language and looks real.

14. How does Dorey suggest to Susan that Susan prove the reality or fantasy of Santa? Ask for something she would not ask her mom for.

15. What does Santa claim he is a symbol for? Accepting on faith.

16. Who baby-sits for Susan when Dorey and Bryan go out? Kris Kringle.

17. What does Susan ask Santa for? House, brother, dad.

18. What present does Bryan offer to Dorey? What does she call him? Engagement ring. Fool.

19. To whom does Bryan give the ring? Kris.

20. Why does Santa get arrested? Hits the old Santa with his cane.

21. Why does the judge wait to sign Kris' commitment papers? Mr. Bedford asks for a formal hearing to prove Santa's sanity.

22. How does Coles show its support for Kris before his hearing? We believe in Santa signs and buttons.

23. Who is Mr. Bedford's first witness? The judge's grandson.

24. Who is Mr. Bedford's second witness? The prosecutor's wife, Mrs. Collins.

25. Who confirms to the Collins children that Kris was the real Santa? Mr. Collins.

26. Why can't Kris make the reindeer fly? They only fly on Christmas Eve.

27. How does Susan convince the Judge that Santa is real? Gives him a dollar bill. In God we Trust.

28. Does Susan get what she wanted from Santa for Christmas? Explain. Yes. Dorey and Bryan marry and will buy the house. Dorey may be pregnant.

Discussion: Answer these questions in complete sentences after you watch the movie.

1. Do you believe parents should allow their children to believe in Santa Claus or should they tell them the truth? Explain.

2. What is the theme of *Miracle on 34th Street?* Which characters help develop the theme?

REEL WRITING

JUST FOR FUN—CHRISTMAS PUNS

A **pun** is a humorous substitution of words that are alike in sound but different in meaning. See if you can recognize the puns which follow:

What do elves learn in school?	The elf-a-bet.
What is the difference between the Christmas Alphabet and the ordinary alphabet?	The Christmas alphabet has no **L**.
What Christmas Carol is a favorite of parents?	Silent Night.
Why does Santa have three gardens?	So he can hoe, hoe, hoe!
What do snowmen eat for breakfast?	Frosted Flakes.
What do you call Santa's helpers?	Subordinate Clauses.
What kind of candle burns longer, a red candle or a green candle?	Neither! Candles burn shorter!
What do you call people who are afraid of Santa Claus?	Claustophobic.
How did Darth Vader know what Luke Skywalker was getting for Christmas?	He felt his presence.
What did Adam say on the day before Christmas?	It's Christmas, Eve!
What song do guests sing at an Eskimo's Christmas party?	Freeze a jolly good fellow!
What do you call a chicken at the North Pole?	Lost.
Does Santa have any money?	No. That's why they call him St. Nickeless!
What do you call it when your Christmas tree explodes?	A tannen-bomb.
What did the sheep say to the shepherd?	Seasons Bleatings!
What did the gingerbread man put on his bed?	A cookie sheet.

KNOCK, KNOCK JOKES

Knock, knock?
Who's there?
Snow.
Snow who?
There's snow business like show business!

Knock, knock?
Who's there?
Wayne.
Wayne who?
Wayne a manger!

Knock, knock?
Who's there?
Donut
Donut who?
Donut open 'til Christmas!

Knock, knock?
Who's there?
Oakham
Oakham who?
Oakham all ye faithful!

Knock, knock?
Who's there?
Rudolph
Rudolph who?
Money is the Rudolph all evil!

Knock, knock?
Who's there?
Igloo
Igloo who?
Igloo knew Suzie like I knew Suzie!

Knock, knock?
Who's there?
Mary
Mary who?
Mary Christmas!

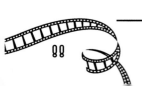

REEL WRITING

WRITING A FILM REVIEW

1. Write a short **summary** of the film, possibly three or four sentences. A summary of the *Joy Luck Club* might read something like this: "The *Joy Luck Club* by Amy Tan is told through a series of vignettes about four mothers in China and their four daughters in America. The film shows the power of the mother-daughter relationship and the transforming power of hope. June is the principal narrator who is about to go to China to meet her twin sisters who were lost for years. The story is told through flashbacks at a party held for June."

2. Give your **opinion** of the film. Be sure to include the movie's strengths and weaknesses. Refer to specific examples or scenes in the movie. For the *Joy Luck Club* you might say, " The film has extraordinary scenery and costumes. The audience learns many details about Chinese culture such as the matchmaking traditions, the importance of being a good cook, and the overwhelming compulsion to sacrifice one's life for a loved one. The dialect of the mothers is in broken English—a blend of Chinese and American language, just as the women live a blend of Chinese and American culture. The hardest part of the movie is following the flashbacks. It takes several stories to realize that they are flashback vignettes. And all the actresses look very much alike."

3. Describe the **character** you like the most or can identify with the most. Describe that person's personality traits. For the *Joy Luck Club*, you might say, "I identify most with the character of Lindo. When the family has to move to find food, she stays behind to honor a marriage contract set up by the parents when she was small. She is a strategist, so she figures out a way to be released from the marriage contract by making up stories about what the ancestors wanted. She honors the contract and her mother, and she gets released to do what she wants—go to America."

4. What do you think is the **theme** or **message communicated** about the film? For the *Joy Luck Club* you might say, "The *Joy Luck Club* is a movie about mother-daughter relationships and inherited traits. Each mother endures hardships in China and comes to America with dreams of a better life for their daughters. However, the daughters grow up and experience many of the same hardships in America that their mothers did in China; only the environment is different. In the end, all persevere and gain new hopes and dreams in America for themselves and for generations to come."

5. What did the film **teach about American culture, other cultures, or historical periods?** For the *Joy Luck Club* you might say, "The film shows the reality of the American dream. The Chinese mothers struggle to gain respect in America. Their daughters benefit from the mothers' struggles and grow as individuals. The daughters become a blend of the best of both cultures, a kind of 'melting pot' like America."

6. Would you **recommend** the movie to someone else? Give the movie a "thumbs up" or a "thumbs down." "The *Joy Luck Club* is a masterpiece, a work of art. It definitely gets two thumbs up."

chapter 6

Women, Warriors, and Waterfalls

The Last of the Mohicans: Setting as Character

OBJECTIVES

- Students will be able to explain how setting affects a story's plot, mood, and conflict.
- Students will create stories based on stereotype settings and imagery exercises.
- Students will read an excerpt of Cooper's novel and compare it to the movie version.
- Students will practice public speaking skills.

NOTES TO THE TEACHER

The *Last of the Mohicans* takes place in the New England colonies during the French and Indian War. Nathaniel, Uncas, and Chingachgook work to keep Alice Munro and her sister Cora alive. The extraordinary scenery is enough to warrant the movie's viewing. The students will learn about James Fenimore Cooper and the French and Indian war, as well.

Last of the Mohicans is rated R for violence and is 122 minutes long.

POSSIBLE PROBLEMS

The movie has many battle scenes between the English army and the Indians, so be sure to preview this one before you show it. The battle scenes are graffic, but not excessively so. You may want to fast forward the scene where Magua kills Col. Munro. Magua cuts out the colonel's heart. The scene is kind of bloody. It begins when the black horse falls on top of Col. Munro. Chapter 23 4:50-5:13.

PROCEDURES

1. **Setting as Character**—Use this handout to show students how a setting can affect a story's plot, mood, and conflict. Students will create stories from stereotype settings.

2. **Creating a Setting as a Character**—Use this handout to do a group activity in which students create a unique setting and set the characters in motion to create stories.

3. **Last of the Mohicans Background Notes**—Use this page to give students information needed to understand the excerpt and movie.

4. **Excerpt from James Fenimore Cooper's *Last of the Mohicans***—Use this handout to introduce students to Fenimore's writing and the characters in the novel and movie.

5. **Viewing Guide for *Last of the Mohicans***—Students answer these questions as they watch the movie.

Name _____

SETTING AS CHARACTER

Settings can be simply a backdrop for the action of a story to take place, or they can be an essential part of the story's mood and conflict. Settings can add depth and richness to a story if they are developed fully. A setting can be so valuable to the story that if almost functions as a character in the story. Dynamic characters who walk in a colorless, shapeless setting offer less entertainment than they could if the setting were more developed.

Unlike characters, settings do not have goals, motivations, or conflict. But a setting can almost have a personality. It can create mood and emotion; it can even initiate or mirror the story's conflict.

Stories which have settings which function almost as characters include disaster stories, war stories, science fiction stories, horror stories, etc. Would *Armageddon* be suspenseful without the meteor hitting earth? Would *Star Wars* be the same story if it were set in the old West? Could *War of the Worlds* have taken place in the desert instead of a populated city? Could Mark Twain have written *Huckleberry Finn* without the Mississippi River?

Setting can also create mood. A horror story usually takes place in an old house where the electricity goes out. An isolated character usually lives at the end of a deserted dirt road. The mood of the setting can mirror the characters' inner setting. A character lives through a great storm as he makes major life decisions. A tender declaration of love is made in a romantic, moon lit garden.

The time and place of a story can also influence the conflict. A story about road rage must take place on busy city street. A story about poverty and human courage seems quite at home during the Great Depression. A story about courage and suffering takes place in wartime.

The following stories might take place in stereotypical settings. Describe the settings in which each might take place.

Murder	Natural disaster
Road rage	Robin Hood
Romantic love scene	Damsel in distress
Rendezvous	Superhero
Ghost story	Brawl
Science fiction	Declaration of love
Swashbuckler	Fight for civil rights

CREATING A SETTING AS A CHARACTER

You will be divided into groups of four or five. You will be writing about a specific place where an incident will occur involving several people. You will invent a story about the conflict and relay the thoughts and feelings of the characters involved. The sentences in bold type are instructions for what you actually write.

1. Your group must select a public place where a variety of people are likely to be found. The place may exist in the present, past, or future. **As a group, list several adjectives or phrases to describe the scene. Everyone needs to write down the list.**

2. Each group member then writes by himself. Imagine you are there in the setting you chose, unnoticed, but observing what is happening in the place to the people. Now focus on one person. What is he/she doing? Is the person alone or waiting for someone else? Is the person talking to anyone? If so, whom? Allow your imagination to really see and hear the scene.

3. **When the place and persons seem vivid, begin writing the scene. Describe what you see, but begin to write the scene through the eyes of** *that person.*

4. Now look out further at the surroundings and people from the eyes of the person you have become. Has anything changed? Have someone else enter into your field of vision. Has the new person always been there, or has he/she just arrived? Have that person walk up to you and begin to talk.

5. **Now continue writing the scene in the first person from your** *original* **person. How do you feel being there? What is it that you want? Who is this person speaking to you? Is he/she a threat or a help to you? Describe his/her actions as well as your own. Describe the setting as well.**

6. Each group member should then read aloud his writing of the scene and discuss what effect the setting has on the characters and the plot.

7. Then the group will present their individual stories to the class. One person will describe the scene which the group set up and read the list of adjectives. Then all members share their stories.

This exercise involves active imaging. It is used to train actors and to encourage creativity. You should see how closely a setting can influence a story's plot. It can add mood and even set a conflict in action.

REEL WRITING

Name _____

LAST OF THE MOHICANS BACKGROUND NOTES—LAZY

1. The Last of the Mohicans takes place in _____ during the French and Indian War. France and England are fighting for _____ of the American territories. The _____ Indians are friendly to England. The _____ Indians are friendly to France.

2. _____ poses as a Mohawk, but is really a Huron.

3. Only three Mohican Indians remain. Chingachgook is the _____ of Uncas and the adopted father of Nathaniel Poe (Hawkeye or Natty Bumppo in the original novel). These men are independent but favor the _____.

4. Three Indian tribes play parts in the film: Mohawk, Huron, and _____.

5. The Munro family consists of Col. Munro (_____), Cora Munro (daughter), and Alice Munro (_____).

6. _____ is the English officer in love with Cora.

LAST OF THE MOHICANS BACKGROUND NOTES

1. The Last of the Mohicans takes place in 1754-1760 during the French and Indian War. France and England are fighting for control of the American territories. The Mohawk Indians are friendly to England. The Huron Indians are friendly to France.

2. Magua poses as a Mohawk, but is really a Huron.

3. Only three Mohican Indians remain. Chingachgook is the father of Uncas and the adopted father of Nathaniel Poe (Hawkeye or Natty Bumppo in the original novel). These men are independent but favor the English.

4. Three Indian tribes play parts in the film: Mohawk, Huron, and Mohican.

5. The Munro family consists of Col. Munro (father), Cora Munro (daughter), and Alice Munro (daughter).

6. Duncan Heyward is the English officer in love with Cora.

EXCERPT FROM JAMES FENIMORE COOPER'S *LAST OF THE MOHICANS*

The following passage comes from Cooper's original novel text. In this passage, you are introduced to Cora, Alice, Duncan Heyward, Magua, and a stranger. Shortly after this passage, the group is attacked by the Huron Indians.

CHAPTER 2
"Sola, sola, wo ha, ho, sola!"—Shakespeare

While one of the lovely beings we have so cursorily presented to the reader was thus lost in thought, the other quickly recovered from the alarm which induced the exclamation, and, laughing at her own weakness, she inquired of the youth who rode by her side:

"Are such specters frequent in the woods, Heyward, or is this sight an especial entertainment ordered on our behalf? If the latter, gratitude must close our mouths; but if the former, both Cora and I shall have need to draw largely on that stock of hereditary courage which we boast, even before we are made to encounter the redoubtable Montcalm."

"Yon Indian is a 'runner' of the army; and, after the fashion of his people, he may be accounted a hero," returned the officer. "He has volunteered to guide us to the lake, by a path but little known, sooner than if we followed the tardy movements of the column; and, by consequence, more agreeably."

"I like him not," said the lady, shuddering, partly in assumed, yet more in real terror. "You know him, Duncan, or you would not trust yourself so freely to his keeping?"

"Say, rather, Alice, that I would not trust you. I do know him, or he would not have my confidence, and least of all at this moment. He is said to be a Canadian too; and yet he served with our friends the Mohawks, who, as you know, are one of the six allied nations. He was brought among us, as I have heard, by some strange accident in which your father was interested, and in which the savage was rigidly dealt by; but I forget the idle tale, it is enough, that he is now our friend."

"If he has been my father's enemy, I like him still less!" exclaimed the now really anxious girl. "Will you not speak to him, Major Heyward, that I may hear his tones? Foolish though it may be, you have often heard me avow my faith in the tones of the human voice!"

"It would be in vain; and answered, most probably, by an ejaculation. Though he may understand it, he affects, like most of his people, to be ignorant of the English; and least of all will he condescend to speak it, now that the war demands the utmost exercise of his dignity. But he stops; the private path by which we are to journey is, doubtless, at hand."

The conjecture of Major Heyward was true. When they reached the spot where the Indian stood, pointing into the thicket that fringed the military road; a narrow and blind path, which might, with some little inconvenience, receive one person at a time, became visible.

"Here, then, lies our way," said the young man, in a low voice. "Manifest no distrust, or you may invite the danger you appear to apprehend."

EXCERPT FROM JAMES FENIMORE COOPER'S *LAST OF THE MOHICANS* PAGE 2

"Cora, what think you?" asked the reluctant fair one. "If we journey with the troops, though we may find their presence irksome, shall we not feel better assurance of our safety?"

"Being little accustomed to the practices of the savages, Alice, you mistake the place of real danger," said Heyward. "If enemies have reached the portage at all, a thing by no means probable, as our scouts are abroad, they will surely be found skirting the column, where scalps abound the most. The route of the detachment is known, while ours, having been determined within the hour, must still be secret."

"Should we distrust the man because his manners are not our manners, and that his skin is dark?" coldly asked Cora.

A stranger appears and wants to ride with them.

The frown which had gathered around the handsome, open, and manly brow of Heyward, gradually relaxed, and his lips curled into a slight smile, as he regarded the stranger. Alice made no very powerful effort to control her merriment; and even the dark, thoughtful eye of Cora lighted with a humor that it would seem, the habit, rather than the nature, of its mistress repressed.

"Seek you any here?" demanded Heyward, when the other had arrived sufficiently nigh to abate his speed; "I trust you are no messenger of evil tidings?"

"Even so," replied the stranger, making diligent use of his triangular castor, to produce a circulation in the close air of the woods, and leaving his hearers in doubt to which of the young man's questions he responded; when, however, he had cooled his face, and recovered his breath, he continued, "I hear you are riding to William Henry; as I am journeying thitherward myself, I concluded good company would seem consistent to the wishes of both parties."

"You appear to possess the privilege of a casting vote," returned Heyward; "we are three, while you have consulted no one but yourself."

"Even so. The first point to be obtained is to know one's own mind. Once sure of that, and where women are concerned it is not easy, the next is, to act up to the decision. I have endeavored to do both, and here I am."

"If you journey to the lake, you have mistaken your route," said Heyward, haughtily; "the highway thither is at least half a mile behind you."

"Even so," returned the stranger, nothing daunted by this cold reception; "I have tarried at 'Edward' a week, and I should be dumb not to have inquired the road I was to journey; and if dumb there would be an end to my calling." After simpering in a small way, like one whose modesty prohibited a more open expression of his admiration of a witticism that was perfectly unintelligible to his hearers, he continued, "It is not prudent for any one of my profession to be too familiar with those he has to instruct; for which reason I follow not the line of the army; besides which, I conclude that a gentleman of your character has the best judgment in matters of wayfaring; I have, therefore, decided to join company, in order that the ride may be made agreeable, and partake of social communion."

EXCERPT FROM JAMES FENIMORE COOPER'S *LAST OF THE MOHICANS* PAGE 3

"A most arbitrary, if not a hasty decision!" exclaimed Heyward, undecided whether to give vent to his growing anger, or to laugh in the other's face. "But you speak of instruction, and of a profession; are you an adjunct to the provincial corps, as a master of the noble science of defense and offense; or, perhaps, you are one who draws lines and angles, under the pretense of expounding the mathematics?"

The stranger regarded his interrogator a moment in wonder; and then, losing every mark of self-satisfaction in an expression of solemn humility, he answered: "Of offense, I hope there is none, to either party: of defense, I make none—by God's good mercy, having committed no palpable sin since last entreating his pardoning grace. I understand not your allusions about lines and angles; and I leave expounding to those who have been called and set apart for that holy office. I lay claim to no higher gift than a small insight into the glorious art of petitioning and thanksgiving, as practiced in psalmody."

"The man is, most manifestly, a disciple of Apollo," cried the amused Alice, "and I take him under my own especial protection. Nay, throw aside that frown, Heyward, and in pity to my longing ears, suffer him to journey in our train. Besides," she added, in a low and hurried voice, casting a glance at the distant Cora, who slowly followed the footsteps of their silent, but sullen guide, "it may be a friend added to our strength, in time of need."

"Think you, Alice, that I would trust those I love by this secret path, did I imagine such need could happen?"

"Nay, nay, I think not of it now; but this strange man amuses me; and if he 'hath music in his soul', let us not churlishly reject his company." She pointed persuasively along the path with her riding whip, while their eyes met in a look which the young man lingered a moment to prolong; then, yielding to her gentle influence, he clapped his spurs into his charger, and in a few bounds was again at the side of Cora. "I am glad to encounter thee, friend," continued the maiden, waving her hand to the stranger to proceed, as she urged her Narragansett to renew its amble. "Partial relatives have almost persuaded me that I am not entirely worthless in a duet myself; and we may enliven our wayfaring by indulging in our favorite pursuit. It might be of signal advantage to one, ignorant as I, to hear the opinions and experience of a master in the art."

"It is refreshing both to the spirits and to the body to indulge in psalmody, in befitting seasons," returned the master of song, unhesitatingly complying with her intimation to follow; "and nothing would relieve the mind more than such a consoling communion. But four parts are altogether necessary to the perfection of melody. You have all the manifestations of a soft and rich treble; I can, by especial aid, carry a full tenor to the highest letter; but we lack counter and bass! Yon officer of the king, who hesitated to admit me to his company, might fill the latter, if one may judge from the intonations of his voice in common dialogue."

"Judge not too rashly from hasty and deceptive appearances," said the lady, smiling; "though Major Heyward can assume such deep notes on occasion, believe me, his natural tones are better fitted for a mellow tenor than the bass you heard."

"Is he, then, much practiced in the art of psalmody?" demanded her simple companion.

Name _____

EXCERPT FROM JAMES FENIMORE COOPER'S *LAST OF THE MOHICHANS* PAGE 4

Answer the following questions about the excerpt in complete sentences:

1. Describe the setting. How many people seem to be involved? Where are they going?

2. How does Alice feel about the Indian guide? Why does she feel this way?

3. Why does Alice want the stranger to join them?

4. How would you describe the writing style? If you made this scene into a movie, what changes would you make?

Name _____

VIEWING GUIDE FOR *LAST OF THE MOHICANS*

Briefly identify each of the following characters:

1. Daniel Day-Lewis .... Hawkeye (Nathaniel Poe)—

2. Madeleine Stowe .... Cora Munro—

3. Russell Means .... Chingachgook—

4. Eric Schweig .... Uncas—

5. Jodhi May .... Alice Munro—

6. Steven Waddington .... Maj. Duncan Heyward—

7. Wes Studi .... Magua—

8. Maurice Roëves .... Col. Edmund Munro—

Answer the following questions as you watch the movie:

1. In what year does the movie open?

2. Who is the author of the book on which the film is based?

3. What war is the backdrop for the movie?

4. What question does Duncan ask Cora?

5. Magua is supposed to be part of which Indian tribe?

6. Who begins the first Indian battle on the way to the fort? Why is the battle such a surprise?

7. Which Indians attacked the British?

8. Why won't Nathaniel bury the Cameron family?

9. Who is Chingachgook?

10. How does Cora feel about the events and the wilderness?

11. Why is Nathaniel arrested?

12. Who wins the battle at Fort Henry?

13. Why does the French general allow Colonel Munro to leave the fort?

Name _____

VIEWING GUIDE FOR *LAST OF THE MOHICANS* PAGE 2

Skip Chapter 23 4:50-5:13. This is where Magua kills Col. Munro. Look for it when the horse falls on the Colonel.

14. Why do the Mohicans leave Cora, Alice, and Duncan at the waterfall?

15. What does the chief say will happen to each of the prisoners?

16. How does Duncan become a martyr?

17. Which characters die by the end of the movie?

18. How does the movie/book get its title?

Discussion questions: Answer these questions after the movie. Use complete sentences.

1. What is the setting of this story? Where does it take place geographically? Could the action have taken place anywhere else? Explain.

2. Where does the story take place, more specifically—the forest, a fort, a home, etc.? What sorts of details are given to us about each place? What attitude or mood is created toward the place by those details?

3. When does the story take place, in terms of time? What period of history, what year, what season, what time of day? In what ways is the time of the story significant to its meaning? How does the time help develop the conflict of the story?

REEL WRITING

Name _____

VIEWING GUIDE FOR *LAST OF THE MOHICANS* PAGE 3

4. What are the other significant aspects of the story's environment—the social, mental, and moral conditions of the characters? How are these conditions revealed to us by details of place and time? How else are they revealed?

5. Are the central characters of the story in conflict or in harmony with the setting? How do you know?

6. In what ways is the setting suggestive or symbolic? How does our knowledge and analysis of the setting contribute to our understanding of the characters, and of the story's meaning as a whole?

VIEWING GUIDE FOR *LAST OF THE MOHICANS*—TEACHER

Briefly identify each of the following characters:

1. Daniel Day-Lewis .... Hawkeye (Nathaniel Poe)—

2. Madeleine Stowe .... Cora Munro—

3. Russell Means .... Chingachgook—

4. Eric Schweig .... Uncas—

5. Jodhi May .... Alice Munro—

6. Steven Waddington .... Maj. Duncan Heyward—

7. Wes Studi .... Magua—

8. Maurice Roëves .... Col. Edmund Munro—

Answer the following questions as you watch the movie:

1. In what year does the movie open? 1757.

2. Who is the author of the book on which the film is based? James Fenimore Cooper.

3. What war is the backdrop for the movie? French and Indian War.

4. What question does Duncan ask Cora? Will she marry him?

5. Magua is supposed to be part of which Indian tribe? Mohawks.

6. Who begins the first Indian battle on the way to the fort? Why is the battle such a surprise? Magua. They thought he was on their side.

7. Which Indians attacked the British? Hurons.

8. Why won't Nathaniel bury the Cameron family? He doesn't want the Indians to know they've been there.

9. Who is Chingachgook? Father of Uncas and adopted father of Nathaniel.

10. How does Cora feel about the events and the wilderness? They are more deeply stirring to her blood than any imagining could possibly have been.

11. Why is Nathaniel arrested? He helps the settlers to leave.

12. Who wins the battle at Fort Henry? The French.

VIEWING GUIDE FOR *LAST OF THE MOHICANS*—TEACHER PAGE 2

13. Why does the French general allow Colonel Munro to leave the fort? Munro promises to return to England. They may leave the fort armed.

Skip Chapter 23 4:50-5:13. This is where Magua kills Col. Munro. Look for it when the horse falls on the Colonel.

14. Why do the Mohicans leave Cora, Alice, and Duncan at the waterfall? All the gunpowder is wet. They promise to return. Nathaniel says to "stay alive!"

15. What does the chief say will happen to each of the prisoners? Magua gets Alice to heal his heart. Duncan goes back to the English. Cora burns in the fire for Magua's children. Nathaniel goes free.

16. How does Duncan become a martyr? He takes Cora's place. He gets burned.

17. Which characters die by the end of the movie? How does each die? Duncan gets burned. Alice jumps off the cliff. Uncas is killed by the Hurons. Magua is killed by Chingachgook. Colonel Munro is killed by Magua.

18. How does the movie/book get its title? Explain. At the end, only Chingachgook is left. His son Uncas was killed.

Discussion questions: Answer these questions after the movie. Use complete sentences.

1. What is the setting of this story? Where does it take place geographically? Could the action have taken place anywhere else? Explain.

2. Where does the story take place, more specifically—the forest, a fort, a home, etc.? What sorts of details are given to us about each place? What attitude or mood is created toward the place by those details?

 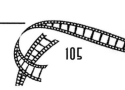

VIEWING GUIDE FOR *LAST OF THE MOHICANS—*TEACHER PAGE 3

3. When does the story take place, in terms of time? What period of history, what year, what season, what time of day? In what ways is the time of the story significant to its meaning? How does the time help develop the conflict of the story?

4. What are the other significant aspects of the story's environment—the social, mental, and moral conditions of the characters? How are these conditions revealed to us by details of place and time? How else are they revealed?

5. Are the central characters of the story in conflict or in harmony with the setting? How do you know?

6. In what ways is the setting suggestive or symbolic? How does our knowledge and analysis of the setting contribute to our understanding of the characters, and of the story's meaning as a whole?

chapter 7

The Dating Game

Sense and Sensibility: Irony and Satire

OBJECTIVES

- Students will be able to identify satire and irony in various kinds of writing.
- Students will perform skits which includes satire and irony.
- Students will practice performance skills.

NOTES TO TEACHER

Sense and Sensibility uses irony and exaggeration to create a satirical story. Jane Austin's story makes fun of the courting practices in England which teach that a woman's success in life is determined by what kind of man she marries. The plot takes many twists and turns as the sisters Elinor and Marianne try to win the love of the men they want to marry.

Sense and Sensibility is rated PG and is 136 minutes long.

POSSIBLE PROBLEMS

None.

PROCEDURES

1. **Satire**—Use this transparency to give definitions to students of satire and the three kinds of irony.

2. **Apply satire definitions**—Find an article on the internet which uses satire to make a point and run it off for the students or make a transparency. Have them explain why the article is satirical. A good article to use is <http://www.stressbuster1.com/pics/kennedy.html>. This article makes fun of Edward Kennedy's expressed desire to help the victims of Hurricane Katrina in Louisiana (August 2005). You may be able to find more current articles in magazines such as the *Onion*, but be careful of content. Satire has a tendency to anger some groups of people and may not be appropriate.

   You may also find a short story which uses satire for the students to analyze. "The Pedestrian" by Ray Bradbury satirizes the extreme use of technology. "Git on Board" in *The Colored Museum* by George Wolfe satirizes slavery and the civil rights movement.

3. **Sense or Sensibility?**—Use this activity to help the students to understand the movie's title.

4. *Sense and Sensibility* **Viewing Guide**—Students answer these questions as they watch the movie.

5. **Quiz for *Sense and Sensibility***—Use this quiz to measure student understanding.

6. **Group Project for *Sense and Sensibility***—Students apply understanding of satire and irony to create group skits. Use the rubric to assign grades to students' projects.

SATIRE

Satire is the use of ridicule to criticize folly or vice.

    Folly is the trait of acting stupidly or rashly; foolishness; craziness.

    Vice is moral weakness; a defect; a fault; an imperfection.

To analyze satire consider:

What/who is being ridiculed or being presented in a ridiculous manner (a system, practice, belief, idea, group, society)?

Which techniques are being utilized to convey this ridicule (analogy, exaggeration, reversal, irony, distortion)?

Irony

Verbal irony—the meaning intended by the speaker is not what the words actually convey; sarcasm.

    Say "You haven't changed a bit" to a person who has gained weight. "I've seen shirts with higher IQs than yours."

Dramatic irony—the audience/reader knows something the character or characters do not know, or character "a" knows something character "b" does not know. The discrepancy creates suspense.

    Example: We know the murderer is behind the door. We know Juliet is not really dead. We know the treasure is not real.

Situational irony—a turn of events that is contrary to what the reader expects to happen; when the event we least expect occurs.

    Example: The strongest man in a shipwreck dies. The couple falls in love and does not get together. The stolen money is counterfeit.

SENSE OR SENSIBILITY?

Take students outside and line them up in front of you in a straight vertical line. Students will step to their right or left depending on their answers to the questions.

1. If you make lists and check things off as you finish them, move to the left.
2. If you don't worry about details as long as the job gets done, move to the right.
3. If you make decisions based on fact, move to the left.
4. If you make decisions based on feelings, move to the right.
5. If you have a strong sense of time, move to the left.
6. If you have trouble sensing time, move to the right.
7. If you are usually on time, move to the left.
8. If you are habitually late, move to the right.
9. If your room is neat and clean, move to the left
10. If your room is messy, move to the right.
11. If you remember names easily, move to the left.
12. If you remember faces more easily, move to the right.
13. If you like math problems, move to the left.
14. If you like English or drama, move to the right.
15. If you have fun without taking risks, move to the left.
16. If you think it's fun to take risks, move to the right.
17. If you keep your furniture the same way, move to the left.
18. If you move your furniture around, move to the right.
19. If you have good self-discipline, move to the left.
20. If you lack self-discipline, move to the right.
21. If you make your bed each day, move to the left.
22. If you leave your bed unmade, move to the right.
23. If you research a problem before solving, move to the left.
24. If you solve a problem by trial and error, move to the right.
25. If you choose friends based on logic, move to the left.
26. If you choose friends based on feelings, move to the right.
27. If you prefer to think your problems out on your own, move to the left.
28. If you prefer to talk out problems or decisions with friends, move to the right.
29. If you are careful whom you fall in love with, move to the left.
30. If you believe in love at first sight, move to the right.

Students who are left of center are ruled by sense.
Students who are right of center are ruled by sensibility (the heart).
The degree to the left or right indicates the degree of sense or sensibility.

Name _____

SENSE AND SENSIBILITY VIEWING GUIDE

Briefly identify each character as you watch the movie:

1. Tom Wilkinson .... Mr. Dashwood—

2. James Fleet .... John Dashwood—

3. Harriet Walter .... Fanny Dashwood—

4. Kate Winslet .... Marianne Dashwood—

5. Emma Thompson .... Elinor Dashwood—

6. Gemma Jones .... Mrs. Dashwood—

7. Emilie François .... Margaret Dashwood—

8. Hugh Grant .... Edward Ferrars—

9. Elizabeth Spriggs .... Mrs. Jennings—

10. Robert Hardy .... Sir John Middleton—

11. Alan Rickman .... Colonel Brandon—

12. Greg Wise .... John Willoughby—

13. Imogen Stubbs .... Lucy Steele—

14. Imelda Staunton .... Charlotte Palmer—

15. Hugh Laurie .... Mr. Palmer—

16. Richard Lumsden .... Robert Ferrars—

Answer these questions as you watch the movie:

1. Why does John Dashwood inherit the entire estate from his father?

2. How much money will the stepmother, Mrs. Dashwood, get each year?

3. Who is the author of the book on which the movie is based?

4. How is Edward Ferras related to Fanny?

5. How does Edward get Margret out of hiding?

6. Why does Mrs. Dashwood postpone her family's move to Sir John Middleton's cottage?

7. Why doesn't Marianne like Edward at first?

8. With whom does Sir John Middleton live? Describe her.

9. Why hasn't Col. Brandon married?

10. How does Marianne meet John Willoughby?

11. Where do Col. Brandon's flowers come from? Where do Willoughby's come from?

12. Which sister plans the budget?

SENSE AND SENSIBILITY VIEWING GUIDE PAGE 2

13. Why does Col.Brandon leave the picnic abruptly?

14. John Willoughby leaves abruptly to go where? What explanation does he give?

15. How does Mr. Palmer treat his wife? Give a quote to explain.

16. What secret does Lucy confess to Elinor?

17. What three people does Mrs. Jennings invite to accompany her to London?

18. Which Mr. Farras attends the ball?

19. Describe Willoughby's ill behavior at the ball.

20. What does John Willoughby return to Marianne with his letter?

21. What news does Mrs. Jennings share with Marianne and Elinor about Willoughby?

22. What connection does Willoughby have to Beth? Who is Beth?

23. Why didn't Willoughby propose to Marianne earlier? Who explains to Elinor?

24. Describe Fanny's reaction to Lucy's secret engagement.

25. Why does Edward loose his fortune?

26. When Marianne is sick, Elinor sends Col. Brandon to get whom?

27. Lucy marries whom?

28. What gift does Col. Brandon send to Marianne?

29. Whom does Elinor marry?

30. Whom does Marianne marry?

Discussion questions: Answer these questions in complete sentences after watching the movie.

1. Which sister is ruled by sense? Which sister is ruled by sensibility? How does the screenwriter exaggerate the traits of each? Give specific examples from the movie.

2. What practice is being satirized by this movie? Explain.

Name _____

SENSE AND SENSIBILITY VIEWING GUIDE PAGE 3

3. Which characters do you find the most comical? Explain.

4. Give an example of dramatic irony from the movie.

5. Give an example of verbal irony from the movie.

6. Give an example of situational irony from the movie.

SENSE AND SENSIBILITY VIEWING GUIDE—TEACHER

Briefly identify each character as you watch the movie:

  1. Tom Wilkinson .... Mr. Dashwood—

12. James Fleet .... John Dashwood—

13. Harriet Walter .... Fanny Dashwood—

14. Kate Winslet .... Marianne Dashwood—

15. Emma Thompson .... Elinor Dashwood—

16. Gemma Jones .... Mrs. Dashwood—

17. Emilie François .... Margaret Dashwood—

18. Hugh Grant .... Edward Ferrars—

19. Elizabeth Spriggs .... Mrs. Jennings—

10. Robert Hardy .... Sir John Middleton—

11. Alan Rickman .... Colonel Brandon—

12. Greg Wise .... John Willoughby—

13. Imogen Stubbs .... Lucy Steele—

14. Imelda Staunton .... Charlotte Palmer—

15. Hugh Laurie .... Mr. Palmer—

16. Richard Lumsden .... Robert Ferrars—

Answer these questions as you watch the movie:

  1. Why does John Dashwood inherit the entire estate from his father? Can't divide the estate between two famililes.

  2. How much money will the stepmother, Mrs. Dashwood, get each year? 500 lbs.

  3. Who is the author on which the movie is based? Jane Austin.

  4. How is Edward Ferras related to Fanny? Brother.

  5. How does Edward get Margret out of hiding? Asks where the source of the Nile River is.

  6. Why does Mrs. Dashwood postpone her family's move to Sir John Middleton's cottage? She recognizes an attraction between Elinor and Edward.

  7. Why doesn't Marianne like Edward at first? He's too sedate. He lacks passion.

  8. With whom does Sir John Middleton live? Describe her. His mother Mrs. Jennings. Very loud and nosey.

  9. Why hasn't Col. Brandon married? The girl he loved was beneath his station. She died.

10. How does Marianne meet John Willoughby? Falls and sprains her ankle. He takes her home.

11. Where do Col. Brandon's flowers come from? Hot house Where do Willoughby's come from? A field.

12. Which sister plans the budget? Elinor.

REEL WRITING

SENSE AND SENSIBILITY VIEWING GUIDE—TEACHER PAGE 2

13. Why does Col.Brandon leave the picnic abruptly? He gets a letter..

14. John Willoughby leaves abruptly to go where? What explanation does he give? London. None.

15. How does Mr. Palmer treat his wife? Give a quote to explain. Very sarcastic. "Please stop."

16. What secret does Lucy confess to Elinor? She's secretly engaged to Edward.

17. What three people does Mrs. Jennings invite to accompany her to London? Elinor, Marianne, Lucy.

18. Which Mr Farras attends the ball? Robert Ferras.

19. Describe Willoughby's ill behavior at the ball. Ignores Marianne and stands by a woman.

20. What does John Willoughby return to Marianne with his letter? Her letters and hair.

21. What news does Mrs. Jennings share with Marianne and Elinor about Willoughby? He is to marry another.

22. What connection does Willoughby have to Beth? Who is Beth? He gets her pregnant. She is the daughter of the woman Col. Brandon loved.

23. Why didn't Willoughby propose to Marianne earlier? Who explains to Elinor? He looses his inheritance because of Beth. His relative throws him out. Col. Brandon.

24. Describe Fanny's reaction to Lucy's secret engagement. She goes crazy. She is not pleased.

25. Why does Edward loose his fortune? Gets Beth pregnant.

26. When Marianne is sick, Elinor sends Col. Brandon to get whom? Mother.

27. Lucy marries whom? Robert Ferras.

28. What gift does Col. Brandon send to Marianne? Piano.

29. Whom does Elinor marry? Edward.

30. Whom does Marianne marry? Col. Brandon.

 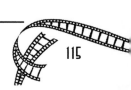

Name _____

QUIZ FOR *SENSE AND SENSIBILITY*

True or False: Decide if each of the following sentences are true or false.

_____ 1. Mr. Dashwood leaves $3000 pounds per year to his second wife and her daughters.

_____ 2. Fanny Dashwood consoles Marianne for the loss of her father.

_____ 3. The author of *Sense and Sensibility* is Jane Austin.

_____ 4. Edward Ferras is the brother of John Dashwood.

_____ 5. Margaret loves to read her atlas.

_____ 6. Mrs. Jennings is the mother of Sir John Middleton.

_____ 7. Marianne thinks Edward is too sedate.

_____ 8. Col. Brandon loved a girl who was a ward of his family.

_____ 9. John Willoughby carries Marianne home when she breaks her leg.

_____ 10. Col. Brandon leaves the picnic because he gets a letter concerning Beth.

_____ 11. Mr. Palmer is sarcastic to his wife Charlotte.

_____ 12. Willoughby marries Miss Gray for her 50,000 pounds per year.

_____ 13. Beth is the daughter of Col. Brandon's lost love.

_____ 14. Fanny is pleased to learn of Lucy's secret engagement to Edward.

_____ 15. Col. Brandon brings Mrs. Dashwood to her sick daughter.

_____ 16. Edward looses his fortune to his brother Robert.

_____ 17. Lucy marries Robert Ferras.

_____ 18. Col. Brandon sends Elinor a piano.

_____ 19. Elinor marries Col. Brandon.

_____ 20. Marianne marries Edward Farras.

Short answer:

21. Give an example from the film of verbal irony.

22. Give an example from the film of dramatic irony.

23. Give an example from the film of situational irony.

24. What practice or idea is being satirized in this film?

25. Which sister represents sense? Which sister represents sensibility? Explain.

REEL WRITING

QUIZ FOR *SENSE AND SENSIBILITY* KEY

1. False

2. False

3. True

4. False

5. True

6. True

7. True

8. True

9. False

10. True

11. True

12. True

13. True

14. False

15. True

16. True

17. True

18. False

19. False

20. False

21. Almost everything Mr. Palmer says to his wife. Marianne asks Fanny, "How did you find the silver?"

22. Lucy confesses her secret engagement to Elinor not knowing Elinor is also in love with Edward.

23. All the girls get the guys in the end. Willoughby marries for money.

24. The dating customs of England. A woman's worth is determined by the marriage she makes.

Name _____

GROUP PROJECT FOR SENSE AND SENSIBILITY

You have learned what satire is. Now as a group, you are to write a skit which satirizes some idea, practice, or group of people. You must include dramatic, verbal, and situational irony in the skit. You do not need to write the script. Merely decide what the skit will be and perform it as an improvisation.

Names of people in the group—

	Weak (4 pts.)	**A**verage (6 pts.)	**G**ood (8 pts.)	**E**xcellent (10 pts.)
Is the practice being satirized clear?				
Dramatic irony included				
Verbal irony included				
Situational irony included				
Well communicated story				

Total Points:_____ **/50**

OBJECTIVES

- Students will read a book which has been made into a movie and look for similarities and differences between the two.
- Students will answer general questions in a reading log format about their books as they read.
- Students will write an essay which compares and contrasts the book and movie.

NOTES TO THE TEACHER

Allow students to choose a novel which was made into a movie. They will read the novel in class and view the movie outside of class. The movies will be viewed outside of class either individually or in groups if several read the same novel.

POSSIBLE PROBLEMS

Since the novels may not be on the school's approved reading list, be sure to get parent approval. Also, some of the movies may be R rated. As long as the parents or guardians approve of their student's choice, the teacher should be free of any problems based on the student's choice.

PROCEDURES

1. **Permission Letter for Book/Movie Project**—At least two weeks before the beginning of the project, send the permission letter home for choice and parent approval. It should be returned with the appropriate signatures.

2. **Reading Log Questions for Book/Movie**—Students spend a week in class reading their novels and answering their reading log questions.

3. **Essay for Book/Movie**—Students view the movie outside of class and write a comparison/contrast essay on the novel/movie.

4. **Essay Evaluation Rubric**—Use this rubric to assign grades to students' essays.

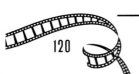

Name _____

PERMISSION LETTER FOR BOOK/MOVIE PROJECT

Dear Parents or Guardian,

During the week of _____, students in the *Film as Literature* class will be reading books which have been made into movies. They will read in class and then answer questions about the portion of the book they read each day. The book must be completed by _____. You may find a list of books made into movies at http://www.skokie.lib.il.us/s_teens/tn_books/tn_booklists/bookfilm.html.

During the following week of _____, each student is to view the movie which was made from his/her book. The viewing of the movie is to be done outside of class—at home or in groups if more than one person reads the same book. Each student will then write an essay which compares and contrasts the book and the movie made from the book.

I need you to help your son or daughter select a book and movie combination. Be sure you can find a copy of the book and a copy of the movie to view. Because the book may not be on the approved reading list for the school district, I need parent approval for the choice. The rating of the movie doesn't matter so long as the parent/guardian approves.

Thanks for your help,

Film Teacher

- -

_____ has my permission to read
(student name)

_____ by _____
(title)   (author)

and then view the movie _____ at home.

_____   _____
(parent or guardian)   (date)

Name _____

ESSAY FOR BOOK/MOVIE

You must write a five paragraph essay which compares the novel which you read to the movie made from it. Your essay must be double spaced in a 12 point font. The essay should be free of errors in spelling, grammar, punctuation, word choice, etc.

The introduction must contain a strategy (anecdote, quote, statistic, rhetorical question, mystery, etc.) and end with a thesis statement.

The three body paragraphs must point out the similarities and differences between the novel and the movie. Be sure to give specific details from each to inform the reader. Write the paper as though the reader has neither seen the movie nor read the book. Give copious details.

In writing a comparison/contrast essay, you may use one of two strategies. You will be considering such details as character development, leaving out characters, combining characters, setting, length of time portrayed, etc.

Strategy one: In the first body paragraph, tell details about the novel. In the second body paragraph, tell details about the movie. In the third body paragraph, tell how both are alike and different.

Strategy two: Choose three main areas to consider. In body paragraph one, describe the first main area in the book and the movie—both similarities and differences. In body paragraph two, describe the second main area in the book and the movie—both similarities and differences. In body paragraph three, do the same for the third main area of consideration.

End the essay with a conclusion. The thesis should be restated in different words. Each body paragraph should be summarized. Then end with a clincher sentence which makes the paper sound finished.

Name _____

READING LOG QUESTIONS FOR BOOK/MOVIE

Each day you will read in class for forty-five minutes and then answer one question based on the portion of the book you have read at that point. For each log entry you must put the title of the book, the author of the book, the page you started on in class, and the page you ended on in class. You may also read outside of class. Your answers may come from any portion of the book you have read to that point, but I need the pages read in class as a point of reference. Each entry must be at least ___ page(s) long and written neatly in paragraph form.

1. What is the basic situation of your book—the main characters, the setting, the conflict?

2. Describe in detail the setting. Does the setting create a mood or help develop the conflict? Explain.

3. Which character do you find the most interesting? Why? Give examples of his appearance, speech, actions, and relationships with others.

4. Does the book contain any irony—verbal, dramatic, or situation? Give examples.

5. Is your book one that will become a classic? Will anyone care about reading it several years from now? Explain.

6. What is the climax of your book? Summarize.

7. Summarize the book's resolution. Are all the loose ends tied up, or does it have a hook resolution? Explain.

8. Do you like the author's type of writing? Do you think you will ever read another book by this author? Why or why not?

Name _____

ESSAY EVALUATION RUBRIC

	Weak (4 pts.)	**A**verage (6 pts.)	**G**ood (8 pts.)	**E**xcellent (10 pts.)
Appearance				
Introduction (development and strategy) and Clear Thesis				
Clear Comparison and Contrast Strategy Used				
Body I (Topic sentence, developed)				
Body II (Topic sentence, developed)				
Body III (Topic sentence, developed)				
Conclusion (Thesis, summary, clincher)				
Sentence structure (Run-ons, fragments)				

Spelling (10 points, five points off for each error)_____

Grammar, punctuation, word choice, other (10 points)_____

Total Points:_____/100

REEL WRITING

Chapter 9

Short Order Story

Fried Green Tomatoes:
Vignettes and Frame Story

OBJECTIVES

- Students will be able to recognize and write vignettes.
- Students will be able to recognize and write frame stories.
- Students will practice listening skills.
- Students will practice performance skills.

NOTES TO THE TEACHER

Fried Green Tomatoes is really two stories. The outer story is about Evelyn and Ninny Threadgoode. Evelyn visits Ninny over a period of several months and Ninny tells her the story of Idgie and Ruth through a series of vignettes. Evelyn gains new courage from the tales and finds that her marriage and life in general are improved. Idgie and Ruth, the women in the inner story, are two women who run a café in the South during the Great Depression years. The movie is a story about the transforming power of frienship.

Fried Green Tomatoes is rated PG 13 and is 136 minutes long.

POSSIBLE PROBLEMS

The movie deals with race relations, so you might want to address the use of dialect (African Americans may be called "colored" or the "N" word). There is a brief appearance of the Klu Klux Klan.

You may want to skip scene 15. A group speaker is teaching Evelyn's group to look at their vaginas. The scene is funny and doesn't really show anything, but it might make some students uncomfortable.

PROCEDURES

1. **Vignettes and Frame Story**—Use this transparency to give students definitions of vignettes and frame stories. Use the **Vignettes and Frame Story Lazy Notes** to give information quickly.

2. **Vignette Examples**—Find examples of vignettes to share with students. Sandra Cisneros' book *House on Mango Street* is my favorite. You could simply read several of the entries aloud to the students. Ask students to write down examples of poetic language and imagery as they listen.

3. *Fried Green Tomatoes* **Viewing Guide**—Students answer these questions as they watch the movie.

4. **Frame Story/Vignette Group Presentation**—Students apply understanding of frame story and vignettes to create a group skit and stories.

5. **Frame Story/Vignette Group Presentation Rubric**—Use this rubric to assign grades to student presentations.

6. **Vignette Rubric**—Use this rubric to assign grades to individual vignettes.

VIGNETTES AND FRAME STORY—LAZY

Vignette

A vignette is a brief sketch, _____, or short-short story. It may tell a _____ story or contribute a portion to a larger work.

Sandra Cisneros is famous for writing vignettes like those in *House on Mango Street.* These vignettes are characterized by the following:

1. _____ language—Similes, metaphors, alliteration, personification, imagery
2. _____ presentation—The narrator flows from one detail to another like a person engaged in conversation
3. First person narrator—The narrator is the _____ and the *I* of the story. Often the narrator is a child.
4. Lack of _____ marks—Only and experienced writer should try this one.
5. Written in present tense—This is not a requirement, but present tense gives _____ to the story.

Frame Story

A frame story is the _____ unifying story within which one or more tales are related. The frame story opens and closes the story and may also appear between several vignettes.

Sometimes the inner vignettes connect to tell a _____ story. Sometimes the inner vignettes tell _____ stories. The frame story flashes back to the inner vignette stories.

Famous frame stories:
1. Chaucer's *Canterbury Tales*—A group of pilgrims tell stories on their _____ to Canterbury.
2. *The Book of One Thousand and One Nights*—Shahrazad narrates _____ to the King over many nights to prevent her own death.
3. *The Princess Bride*—A grandfather tells his grandson the story of Princess Buttercup and her _____.
4. *Wuthering Heights*—The maid tells the _____ of Heathcliff and Catherine.
5. *Forest Gump*—Forest tells various people his life story as they sit on a _____.
6. *Joy Luck Club*—June is about to go to China to visit her lost _____. The stories of four Chinese mothers and their American daughters are told through a series of _____.

VIGNETTES AND FRAME STORY

Vignette

A vignette is a brief sketch, narrative, or short-short story. It may tell a separate story or contribute a portion to a larger work.

Sandra Cisneros is famous for writing vignettes like those in *House on Mango Street*. These vignettes are characterized by the following:

1. Poetic language—Similes, metaphors, alliteration, personification, imagery
2. Stream of conscious presentation—The narrator flows from one detail to another like a person engaged in conversation
3. First person narrator—The narrator is the main character and the *I* of the story. Often the narrator is a child.
4. Lack of quotation marks—Only and experienced writer should try this one.
5. Written in present tense—This is not a requirement, but present tense gives immediacy to the story.

Frame Story

A frame story is the outer unifying story within which one or more tales are related. The frame story opens and closes the story and may also appear between several vignettes.

Sometimes the inner vignettes connect to tell a unified story. Sometimes the inner vignettes tell unconnected stories. The frame story flashes back to the inner vignette stories.

Famous frame stories:
1. Chaucer's *Canterbury Tales*—A group of pilgrims tell stories on their journey to Canterbury.
2. *The Book of One Thousand and One Nights*—Shahrazad narrates fairy tales to the King over many nights to prevent her own death.
3. *The Princess Bride*—A grandfather tells his grandson the story of Princess Buttercup and her farm boy.
4. *Wuthering Heights*—The maid tells the love story of Heathcliff and Catherine.
5. *Forest Gump*—Forest tells various people his life story as they sit on a park bench.
6. *Joy Luck Club*—June is about to go to China to visit her lost twin sisters. The stories of four Chinese mothers and their American daughters are told through a series of flashbacks.

Name _____

FRIED GREEN TOMATOES VIEWING GUIDE

Briefly identify each character as you watch the movie:

1. Kathy Bates . . . . Evelyn Couch—

2. Mary Stuart Masterson . . . . . Idgie Threadgoode—

3. Mary-Louise Parker . . . . . Ruth Jamison—

4. Jessica Tandy . . . . . Ninny Threadgoode—

5. Cicely Tyson . . . . . Sipsey—

6. Chris O'Donnell . . . . . Buddy Threadgoode—

7. Stan Shaw . . . . . Big George—

8. Gailard Sartain . . . . Ed Couch—

9. Tim Scott . . . . Smokey Lonesome—

10. Gary Basaraba . . . . . Grady Kilgore—

11. Richard Riehle . . . . Reverend Scroggins—

12. Raynor Scheine . . . . .Curtis Smoote—

13. Nick Searey . . . . . Frank Bennett—

Answer these questions as you watch the movie:

1. Whom are Evelyn and Ed Couch visiting at the nursing home?

2. Where is Mrs. Cleo Threadgoode from?

3. Why doesn't Idgie want to come downstairs for the wedding?

4. Who is Buddy's oyster?

5. What happens to Buddy's lake according to his story?

6. How does Buddy die?

7. How does Idgie react to Buddy's death?

8. What kind of meetings does Evelyn attend?

9. What does Idgie tell Frank Bennett her name is?

10. How does Ruth get Idgie to leave the gambling game?

11. What do Ruth and Idgie throw from the train?

12. Why is Idgie called the "bee charmer"?

Skip Scene 15. It starts when the speaker passes out mirrors to Evelyn's group.

Name _____

FRIED GREEN TOMATOES VIEWING GUIDE   PAGE 2

13. Why won't Ruth invite Idgie in when Idgie comes to visit?

14. What does Ruth's letter say to get Idgie to come and get her?

15. What convinces Frank to let his wife go with Idgie?

16. What does Mrs. Threadgoode think might be wrong with Evelyn?

17. What was wrong with Albert, Ninny's son?

18. What do Ruth and Idgie do to earn a living?

19. Why does the Klu Klux Klan whip Big George?

20. Who gets killed during the church play?

21. Which character does Curtis Smoote think killed Frank?

22. What promise does Idgie make to Ruth about Frank?

23. What does Evelyn say about crashing into the parked car several times?

24. How does Buddy lose his arm?

25. What is Buddy's nickname?

26. Who is arrested for Frank Bennett's murder?

27. Which character gets Idgie declared innocent of the murder?

28. What book does the Reverend use to swear in instead of a Bible?

29. What story is Idgie telling when Ruth dies?

30. Why does Evelyn decide to build the wall back in her house?

31. Who really kills Frank?

32. What happens to Frank's body?

33. What does Sipsey say is the secret to the great barbecue?

34. Why did Idgie go on trial?

35. How does Evelyn figure out who Ninny really is?

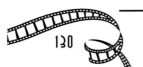

Name _____

FRIED GREEN TOMATOES VIEWING GUIDE PAGE 3

Discussion questions: Answer these questions in complete sentences after you watch the movie.

1. In what ways do Ninny's stories inspire Evelyn?

2. What is the outer frame story? Who are the principal characters?

3. What is the inner story? Who are the principal characters?

4. What is ironic about the ending of the Frank Bennett murder story?

FRIED GREEN TOMATOES VIEWING GUIDE—TEACHER

Briefly identify each character as you watch the movie:

1. Kathy Bates . . . . . . Evelyn Couch—
2. Mary Stuart Masterson . . . . . Idgie Threadgoode—
3. Mary-Louise Parker . . . . . Ruth Jamison—
4. Jessica Tandy . . . . . Ninny Threadgoode—
5. Cicely Tyson . . . . . Sipsey—
6. Chris O'Donnell . . . . . Buddy Threadgoode—
7. Stan Shaw . . . . . Big George—
8. Gailard Sartain . . . . Ed Couch—
9. Tim Scott . . . . Smokey Lonesome—
10. Gary Basaraba . . . . . Grady Kilgore—
11. Richard Riehle . . . . Reverend Scroggins—
12. Raynor Scheine . . . . . Curtis Smoote—
13. Nick Searey . . . . . Frank Bennett—

Answer these questions as you watch the movie:

1. Whom are Evelyn and Ed Couch visiting at the nursing home? Ed's Aunt Vesta.
2. Where is Mrs. Cleo Threadgoode from? Whistle Stop.
3. Why doesn't Idgie want to come downstairs for the wedding? Wearing a dress.
4. Who is Buddy's oyster? Idgie.
5. What happens to Buddy's lake according to his story? Froze and ducks flew away with it.
6. How does Buddy die? Foot caught in train rails—run over by a train.
7. How does Idgie react to Buddy's death? Stays out by the river.
8. What kind of meetings does Evelyn attend? Marriage saving meetings.
9. What does Idgie tell Frank Bennett her name is? Tawanda.
10. How does Ruth get Idgie to leave the gambling game? Takes her money.
11. What do Ruth and Idgie throw from the train? Throw food to the poor.
12. Why is Idgie called the "bee charmer"? She gets honey from a bee hive. Has bees all over her and doesn't get tung.

Skip Scene 15. It starts when the speaker passes out mirrors to Evelyn's group.

FRIED GREEN TOMATOES VIEWING GUIDE—TEACHER   PAGE 2

13. Why won't Ruth invite Idgie in when Idgie comes to visit? Ruth has a black eye.

14. What does Ruth's letter say to get Idgie to come and get her? Quotes the book of Ruth from the Bible.

15. What convinces Frank to let his wife go with Idgie? Big George's knife.

16. What does Mrs. Threadgoode think might be wrong with Evelyn? Change of life. Needs harmones.

17. What was wrong with Albert, Ninny's son? Probably retarded. Lived only 30 years.

18. What do Ruth and Idgie do to earn a living? Open Whistle Stop Café.

19. Why does the Klu Klux Klan whip Big George? He helps Idgie cook.

20. Who gets killed during the church play? Frank Bennett

21. Which character does Curtis Smoote think killed Frank? Idgie.

22. What promise does Idgie make to Ruth about Frank? Frank Bennett will never bother you again.

23. What does Evelyn say about crashing into the parked car several times? I'm older and have better insurance.

24. How does Buddy lose his arm? Train runs over it.

25. What is Buddy's nickname? Stump.

26. Who is arrested for Frank Bennett's murder? Idgie.

27. Which character gets Idgie declared innocent of the murder? Reverend.

28. What book does the Reverend use to swear in instead of a Bible? Moby Dick.

29. What story is Idgie telling when Ruth dies? The ducks carrying away the frozen lake.

30. Why does Evelyn decide to build the wall back in her house? She wants Ninny to come live with her. She needs a room for Ninny.

31. Who really kills Frank? Sipsey.

32. What happens to Frank's body? Cooked into barbeque.

33. What does Sipsey say is the secret to the great barbecue? The secret's in the sauce.

34. Why did Idgie go on trial? Sipsey or Big George would be found guilty.

35. How does Evelyn figure out who Ninny really is? Finds honey on Ruth's grave.

FRIED GREEN TOMATOES VIEWING GUIDE—TEACHER PAGE 3

Discussion questions: Answer these questions in complete sentences after you watch the movie.

1. In what ways do Ninny's stories inspire Evelyn?

1. What is the outer frame story? Who are the principal characters?

1. What is the inner story? Who are the principal characters?

1. What is ironic about the ending of the Frank Bennett murder story?

REEL WRITING

Name _____

FRAME STORY/VIGNETTE GROUP PRESENTATION

You will be divided into groups of four or five. You will decide as a group what your frame story will be. Then each person will write his/her own vignette.

You may perform the frame story as an improvisation, but the vignettes must be written out. Each person will read his/her vignette as you move through the frame story.

Possible frames might be a class reunion, people caught in an elevator, people caught in a disaster or wreck (*Lost*), people at a party, people in jail, etc.

Vignette requirements:

The vignette must be about 300-500 words. Concentrate on details. This is not a narrative essay. There will be neither an introduction nor a conclusion. You start in the middle of the story. Show, don't tell. Think of this as a dramatic scene in prose form. Use words to create images that appeal to the senses. Let your characters speak. Use dialogue.

The vignette may be neatly hand-written on one side of the page only or it may be typed double-spaced in a 12 point font.

Name _____

FRAME STORY/VIGNETTE GROUP PRESENTATION RUBRIC

Names of group members:

ELEMENTS	**W**eak (4 pts.)	**A**verage (6 pts.)	**G**ood (8 pts.)	**E**xcellent (10 pts.)
Frame story introduces series of vignettes				
Frame story connects vignettes				
Frame story concludes series of vignettes				
Quality of performance (effort)				

Total Points:_____/50

REEL WRITING

Name _____

VIGNETTE RUBRIC

Names of group members:

ELEMENTS	**W**eak (4 pts.)	**A**verage (6 pts.)	**G**ood (8 pts.)	**E**xcellent (10 pts.)
Length and Neatness				
Images and Sensory Detains				
Use of Dialogue				
Showing Characters				

Spelling (10 points, 5 points off for each error) _____

Grammar, punctuation, word choice, other (10 points)_____

Total Points:_____**/60**

OBJECTIVES

- Students will be able to identify the characteristics of memoirs and use them to construct a memoir story.
- Students will practice reading aloud.

NOTES TO THE TEACHER

Riding in Cars with Boys is the story of Beverly Donofrio's life from age 15 to 35. She gets pregnant out of wedlock and is forced by her parents to get married. She must delay her education dreams to care for a baby and husband who has learning disabilities and drug problems.

Riding in Cars with Boys is rated PG 13 for thematic elements, drug, and sexual content. The film is 131 minutes long.

POSSIBLE PROBLEMS

The film deals with some delicate issues—teen pregnancy and drug use. Beverly and Ray get pregnant and married at 15. Ray has learning disabilities and tries to self medicate by experimenting with drugs. But the message is clear: Unprotected sex and drug use can wreck a person's life. The issues are handled quite tastefully. The movie is also very humorous and shows how a person's perseverance can turn even the most difficult situations around.

PROCEDURES

1. **Free Write**—Have students write for ten minutes about a childhood memory and then have read aloud to the class.

2. **Memoirs**—Use this sheet to give students the definition and characteristics of memoirs. Students will begin to keep journal which will be used to write a memoir.

3. **Show and Tell**—Students bring an item to class which has great meaning to them. Seat the class in a circle and have each student tell the story behind his object. The student should tell how he got the object and why is has significance to him. Then the teacher tells the students that they have all told a memoir story.

4. **"This Little Light of Mine"**—Use this story as an example of a memoir.

5. *Riding in Cars with Boys* **Viewing Guide**—Students will answer questions as they watch the movie.

6. **Memoirs Rubric**—Use this rubric to assign grades to students' memoirs.

Name _____

MEMOIRS

A memoir is a piece of autobiographical writing, usually shorter in length than an autobiography. The memoir captures certain moments, events, or highlights of a person's life. The memoir is more concentrated on capturing the emotion and sensory details of the events, instead of simply recording them.

- Focuses on brief periods of time or series of events
- Uses narrative structure
- Has a fictional quality but is based on truth
- May be "faction"—facts mixed with fictionalized details (like conversations)
- Infers meaning of events
- Often deals with crisis or survival events

Assignment: For a period of at least a week, keep a journal in which you record things that have happened to you. You may write it as a diary or simply as a list of snatches of things which occurred. Write down random thoughts, bits of conversation, events, etc.

You will turn in your journal for daily points. You must write at least ___ page(s) for each day. Put the date for each entry.

You will use at least one of your entries to expand into a memoir story. Maybe take an event and describe the scene completely. Show what the scene looks like. Describe the characters involved. Write the events and dialogue. Tell the story. You are the narrator, so use first person. You may be the central character or merely the narrator telling something you saw.

The memoir must be at least two neatly handwritten pages or typed in a 12 point font. Make sure to use correct punctuation, grammar, spelling, etc.

THIS LITTLE LIGHT OF MINE

By Brian Smithson

Three boys were peering at me over the gate of my compound. "Hey, what are you cooking, white man?"

"Small children."

I wasn't cooking. The flaming heap in my front yard was fed by old bank statements, Peace Corps pay stubs, and other documents I didn't feel should be available for public consumption in the neighborhood trash pile/yard sale. I'd be leaving Thursday, and already the stress was starting to mount.

"That's not a child! That's paper. When will you cook something? We're hungry."

"How about Sunday?"

"Sunday? Really? Gee, thanks, Mister!"

I smiled. "See you then!"

*****

Moving is difficult. Moving in Africa is really difficult.

First of all, your neighbors pick up the scent very early on. As early as six months ago, I'd been approached by the man who lives behind me about him buying my "little things" when I left. Around the same time, the landlady asked about buying all my furniture. And as the final few months rolled along, other people began to ask for a "souvenir" of my stay. The logic of this is annoyingly sound in some cases, not so much in others.

"You're going back to America, right? There you can buy a new computer very easily, but here it's difficult. So leave me the laptop, okay?"

But I figured it out, more or less. Three or four friends got nice gifts, by Cameroonian standards anyway: a sleeping bag, an expensive grammar book, a gas bottle. The furniture went to the landlady. I then gave all my miscellaneous stuff and excess clothing to my church. This saved me a lot of grief, especially from the random people who would wake me up at 5 AM to ask for a *cadeau*. "Sorry! Gave it to the church!"

But getting rid of stuff is only one of the tedious tasks the departing volunteer must undertake. There's also the preponderance of Peace Corps paperwork. Close out your water bill, sign a form. Pay your final rent, sign a form. Get the power cut, sign a . . . Well, we'll get to that.

*****

I headed to the offices of the Cameroonian power company, SONEL, a full week in advance of my departure. They are notoriously negligent about being in their office, and they refuse to work when the power is cut (define "irony").

I asked when they could cut the power, and they said that day. When I explained that I still had a week left at post, though, the head of the office told me he'd send his assistant to cut the juice on the next Wednesday. He asked if I had the receipt from when I had opened the account and left my deposit, and I explained that I thought I had lost

THIS LITTLE LIGHT OF MINE
PAGE 2

it. He replied that I wouldn't get the money back then, too bad. This was about $40 I'd be out. Still, for forty bucks I could get my power cut, get my form signed, and get out of Abong-Mbang. At least an even trade.

Fast-forward seven days. I arrived at the SONEL office early in the morning, and I found the deputy.

"Look, I found my receipt, so I can get my deposit back! So can you come cut the power today?"

He looked crestfallen. "Um . . . the guy with the . . . *screwdriver* is on his way back from Bertoua. I can't take your counter and cut the power until . . . 4 PM this afternoon."

I didn't think to ask why the power company only had one screwdriver. "Okay. I'll wait for you at the house."

I left mildly annoyed, since when you're leaving a place you'll probably never see again, you kind of want to be out with friends or getting your stuff together or seeing the sights one last time. Instead, I was reading *Island of the Blue Dolphins* on a bare foam mattress and looking at my watch like a teenager forced to go to his third cousin's ballet recital. The man never came.

*****

The next day was Thursday. D-Day. *Départ définitif.*

The landlady dropped in early. She enlisted the aid of the student bruisers who live next door to move all the furniture out. Around 8 AM, I put a stop to the pillage so that I could go to the SONEL office once more and find out why they had stood me up the previous day. A man outside the building informed me that no one would be there that day; they had gone *en brousse*. This was unacceptable. And I declared war.

I quickly found a moto taxi. It was a bumpy ride through the pre-storm mist, but we found the SONEL guys in less than fifteen minutes. The truant deputy hung from a utility pole while his boss gazed up from the ground offering random nuggets of know-how. Their blue hardhats and the crowd of bored villagers staring on suddenly made me feel better about the curious looks *I* got as a white man in a Power Rangers helmet on the back of a motorcycle.

I got off the bike. "Good morning, SONEL! I waited for you yesterday like we had arranged! What happened?"

They ignored me.

"It's like that, is it? Well, as I explained to you a week ago, I must leave Abong-Mbang today, and I can't do so until you cut my power."

The boss finally looked at me, with derision. "Will you go away? We're trying to work here."

"Yeah. Too bad you didn't want to work yesterday like you had promised me." I paid my moto driver his fare. "I'm not going anywhere." I didn't want to annoy them too much, at least not at first, so I went up to introduce myself to the homeowner whose property they were currently standing on and over. As the deputy descended, though, I approached once again. They ignored me and walked on to a pole a few mud huts away.

THIS LITTLE LIGHT OF MINE
PAGE 3

I followed them then set my moto helmet on the ground and sat on it. As the deputy scurried up the utility pole, I asked, "So, again. Where were you yesterday? I waited at our appointed time, and you never showed up."

The boss scowled. "We don't owe you an explanation! We're serving our customers here."

"Oh, and what am I, then?"

"Will you please go away? We're working, and you're really annoying us with your endless chatter!"

I smiled. "Oh, I can do better than endless chatter." I cleared my throat and began: "Ninety-nine bottles of beer on the wall, ninety-nine bottles of beer . . . ."

"Stop it!"

". . . . Take one down, and pass it around, ninety-eight bottles of beer on the wall."

"Go away!"

"Ninety-eight bottles of beer on the wall, ninety-eight bottles of beer . . . ."

"What has Cameroon gained from your being here?"

". . . . Take one down, and pass it around . . . ."

Most of the village's fifty or so inhabitants had gathered to see the spectacle by this point. Bare-footed men, pot-bellied children, and wizened old women stared on in a mixture of mirth, annoyance, and shock as the White Man harassed the Big Men from the City. I tried to get them involved to some small success with interjections such as, "Let's do the eighties! Eighty-nine bottles of beer on the wall, eighty-nine bottles of beer . . . ."

Reactions ranged from "Akié!" to "Hey, it's a white guy singing!" to "Guess we're going to be eating white man for dinner tonight." At one point, a village adolescent asked if I wanted a guitar to accompany me. "Sure, why not? On to the seventies!"

I got to seventy-four bottles of beer before the SONEL men would acknowledge me.

"Look. If you'll just wait at the office, we'll deal with the problem there."

"But I need to leave today."

"We can't cut your power today. There's a part we need in Bertoua that won't be back until Monday."

"Is it the screwdriver?"

"No."

THIS LITTLE LIGHT OF MINE
PAGE 4

"So you're telling me that it is completely impossible to cut my power until Monday. Correct?"

"Yes. Now go away."

By this point, the man with the guitar had arrived. SONEL moved on to another pole, and I knew I had better get back to town soon. But the villagers looked on with expectant stares. I didn't want to disappoint them, so I gave them my best rendition of "Let It Be," "No Woman, No Cry," and "We Are the World." The SONEL guys seemed to work surprisingly fast and they rapidly receded into the distance.

****

I was not going to let them win. I knew why they were giving me the run-around: They wanted to *bouffe* the $40 they owned me for my deposit. So I went to the authorities and pleaded my case at the *gendarmerie*. The *chef de brigade* gave me the typical Cameroonian shocked and indignant surprise when confronted with a tale of corruption ("They did *what*?") and agreed to accompany me to the SONEL office.

By the time we got there, the boss and the deputy were back from their musical mission into the wilds. At sight of my new gendarme friend, the boss's temples trembled in what could only have been rage. The gendarme asked, "Can we just arrange something so this man's account can be closed and he can leave today?"

"No, sir. It is *completely* impossible! There's a part in Bertoua that won't be in until Monday!"

I gave on open-handed gesture. "If it's a calculator, I've got one at my house."

The boss's temple pulsated even faster. "Excuse me, but SONEL has *lots* of money! We don't need your . . . calculator!" He then turned to the gendarme. "Do you *hear* this kind of language?"

Eventually, we came to a decision. The SONEL guy would send the deputy to take the counter from my house. He would write down the reading so that he could figure out the final bill. Then he would sign my Peace Corps form saying I had closed my account. The landlady would come back on Monday and get my $40 minus my final bill. She would send it to me in Yaoundé. I knew I'd never see that money, but what's $40 in comparison to a return to life in the First World? I told the SONEL boss that I was going to make a copy of the receipt from when I opened the account and that I'd be back soon.

When I came back, it was as if a miracle had occurred. Boss man produced a calculator and proceeded to tabulate my final bill based on the counter reading. He then subtracted this amount from my deposit. Then, as if my magic, he *gave me back my money*. I'm not sure whether the magic bullet was the gendarme or the Xeroxed bill, but it worked. I thanked him, repressed the urge to serenade him once again, and left.

*****

It was now late afternoon. Still, I mustered as much speed as possible to get my six items of luggage to the *gare routière* to get a bush taxi and to get the hell out of Abong-Mbang. I negotiated with the one-armed baggage handler for how much I'd pay to have my stuff transported, bought my ticket, then watched the sun melt away into the jungle.

THIS LITTLE LIGHT OF MINE
PAGE 5

As a response to recent nighttime road banditry, Peace Corps has recently outlawed travel after dark. I knew that if I left then, I'd arrive well into the night, and the last thing I wanted to do before my Close of Service was to cause a scandal. So I called to ask permission.

I got Dr. Sammy, the head of he education program. "Oh, no! There is no use traveling at night! You should just come tomorrow!"

"But, Dr. Sammy, I don't have any furniture in my house! I can't stay there."

"You can stay at a hotel! We will reimburse you!"

So my final night at post, which should've been my first night in Yaoundé, I spent drinking beers with the gendarme who had helped me earlier in the day and then lying in an uncomfortable bed, swatting mosquitoes, and wondering what other fun little skin infections I might be picking up. I left the next morning.

[Brian Smithson spent two years in the Peace Corps teaching English in a village school in Abong-Mbang, Cameroon.]

Name _____

RIDING IN CARS WITH BOYS VIEWING GUIDE

Briefly identify each character as you watch the movie:

1. Drew Barrymore .... Beverly Donofrio—

2. Steve Zahn .... Ray Hasek—

3. Adam Garcia .... Jason—

4. Brittany Murphy .... Fay Forrester—

5. James Woods .... Mr. Leonard Donofrio—

6. Lorraine Bracco .... Mrs. Teresa Donofrio—

7. Rosie Perez .... Shirley Perro—

8. Sara Gilbert .... Tina Barr—

9. Peter Facinelli .... Tommy Butcher—

Discussion questions: Answer these questions in complete sentences after you watch the movie:

1. What is the outer frame story? Who narrates it?

2. Do you think that Beverly should have married Ray simply because she was pregnant? Does the time period have anything to do with her decision?

3. Why does Ray "forget" so much? How much is his fault and how much is the fault of his learning disability? Explain.

4. Does Beverly love Ray? Cite examples from the movie to support your answer.

5. Is Beverly a good mother? Does she change during the movie? Cite specific examples to explain your answer.

6. Why is Ray's leaving the "best thing" he could do for Jason as a father?

Name _____

RIDING IN CARS WITH BOYS VIEWING GUIDE   PAGE 2

7. Why does Jason tell on his mother for drying marijuana? How does she react when he confesses to her? Why do you think he confesses?

8. In what ways is Beverly and Jason's mother/son relationship typical and in what ways is it not typical? What do you think shapes the relationship?

9. Describe Beverly and Fay's relationship. Are they a good influence on each other or a bad influence? Explain.

10. Describe Ray's second wife in the trailer scene. How do we know she is not pleased with her visitors?

11. What does Ray give Jason when they meet at the trash can? What does this tell us about Ray's feelings for Jason?

12. What advice does Ray give Jason about women? How does Jason apply this advice to his mom?

13. Beverly tells Jason that he's not what went wrong in her life; he's what saved her. Do you agree or disagree with her statement? Explain.

14. Explain the symbolism of the movie's title *Riding in Cars with Boys*. Who are the boys she rides with? What does the "ride" represent? What song frames the whole story?

Name _____

MEMOIR RUBRIC

	Weak (4 pts.)	**A**verage (6 pts.)	**G**ood (8 pts.)	**E**xcellent (10 pts.)
Neatness and Length				
Clear Representation of Scene				
Tells a Story				
Dialogue				
Importance of Event				

Spelling (10 points, five points off for each error) _____

Grammar, punctuation, word choice, other (10 points)_____

Journal entries attached for six days (30 points)_____

Total Points:_____/100

OBJECTIVES

- Students will make predictions and test them against a video text.
- Students will draw conclusions about missionary movements.
- Students will skim a text to find relevant information.

NOTES TO THE TEACHER

The movie *Hawaii* (1966) based on James Michener's novel will teach students about the early history of the islands. Hawaii was a tropical paradise visited occasionally by ship traders. In 1820 the first Christian missionaries arrived, seven married couples. The story covers 1820-1840. We follow closely Jerusha and Abner Hale, one of the original couples, as they witness to Queen Malama.

Hawaii is rated not rated but would probably receive a PG 13 rating today. The film is 161 minutes long.

POSSIBLE PROBLEMS

In the early years the Hawaiian women would swim out to the boats to meet the sailors with naked breasts. The nudity is very brief. When Queen Malama passes a new law, the women stop the practice. Encourage the students to be mature and to think of the film as a documentary. I had absolutely no problems with my students.

PROCEDURES

1. **Brainstorm Historical Events**—Divide students into pairs and ask them to create a list of five events from the past five years which could be made into movies. Share the lists with the class.

2. **Free Write**—Students write for ten minutes on the topic *Hawaii* and share writing aloud.

3. **Brainstorm Hawaiian Facts**—Divide students into pairs. Each pair comes up with a list of possible facts about Hawaii. The list might include items from these categories: language, history, religion, customs, climate, industry, agriculture, etc. Students will use these lists after viewing of *Hawaii*. They will place a *check* beside items which were proven *true* in the movie, an *X* beside items which were proven *false* in the movie, and a line (—) beside items which were not found in the movie so the students *can't tell*.

4. *Hawaii* **Viewing Guide**—Students will answer these questions while watching the movie.

5. *Hawaii* **Test**—Students will demonstrate mastery of the information presented in the movie.

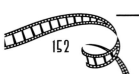

Name _____

HAWAII VIEWING GUIDE

Briefly identify each character as you watch the movie:

1. Julie Andrews . . . . Jerusha Bromley Hale—

2. Mac von Sydow . . . . Abner Hale—

3. Richard Harris . . . . .Rafer Hoxworth—

4. Gene Hackman . . . . Rev. John Whipple—

5. Carroll O'Connor . . . .Charles Bromley—

6. Jocelyne LaGarde . . . . Queen Malama—

7. Manu Tupou . . . . Keoki—

8. Ted Nobriga . . . . Kelolo—

9. Elizabeth Logue . . . . Noelani—

10. Lou Antonio . . . Rev. Abraham Hewlett—

11. Lokelani S. Chicarell . . . Lliki—

Answer these questions as you watch the movie:

1. What was the home of the gods called?

2. Why did the Hawaiians leave their former home?

3. What does Keoki ask for in 1819?

4. What must Abner Hale do before he can be sent as a missionary to Hawaii?

5. How old is Jerusha?

6. Who is she in love with?

7. Why do the Bromley's think Jerusha will be interested in marrying Hale?

8. What happens to Jerusha's letters from Capt. Hoxworth?

9. How does Hale react when Jerusha tells him about Capt. Hoxworth?

10. Why does Hale hit Jerusha on the ship?

11. Who does Keoki swim out to meet from the ship?

12. To whom is Malama married?

13. Who is Noelani?

14. Why does Jerusha faint when she is teaching Queen Malama?

15. Why does Jerusha rescue the Hawaiian baby?

16. Whom do the sailors try to kidnap? Who saves her?

17. Who is the captain of the visiting ship? How does he react when he sees Jerusha?

Name _____

HAWAII VIEWING GUIDE PAGE 2

18. Why does Hale ask Queen Malama for land?

19. According to Keoki, how many kinds of adultery are there? Give some examples.

20. Why does Abner refuse the help of the midwives? Was this a wise decision? Explain.

21. Who is the first member of Hale's church?

22. What are some of the rules which Malama's new law decrees?

23. Who sets the church on fire? Why?

24. Whom does Hoxworth take with him when he leaves?

25. What news does Jerusha's letter bring?

26. Why is Abraham Hulet banned from the church?

27. What teaching by Keoki angers Hale?

28. Why won't Hale make Keoki a preacher?

29. Why does Malama call for Hale and Jerusha when she dies?

30. What causes the wind to start?

31. What does Kololo do to himself after Malama dies?

32. What happens to Malama's bones?

33. What happens to Keoki's baby? Why?

34. Why aren't Hawaiians used as slaves?

35. Why is measles so deadly to the Hawaiians?

36. Who dies at the beach?

37. What does Hoxworth bring Jerusha as a gift?

38. Why can't Hale accept the gift? How does Hoxworth react?

39. Where does Hale send his children? Why?

40. Who offers to help Hale continue his work?

HAWAII VIEWING GUIDE—TEACHER

Briefly identify each character as you watch the movie:

1. Julie Andrews . . . . Jerusha Bromley Hale—
2. Mac von Sydow . . . . Abner Hale—
3. Richard Harris . . . . .Rafer Hoxworth—
4. Gene Hackman . . . . Rev. John Whipple—
5. Carroll O'Connor . . . .Charles Bromley—
6. Jocelyne LaGarde . . . . Queen Malama—
7. Manu Tupou . . . . Keoki—
8. Ted Nobriga . . . . Kelolo—
9. Elizabeth Logue . . . . Noelani—
10. Lou Antonio . . . Rev. Abraham Hewlett—
11. Lokelani S. Chicarell . . . Lliki—

Answer these questions as you watch the movie:

1. What was the home of the gods called? Bora Bora.
2. Why did the Hawaiians leave their former home? New god is asking for human sacrifice.
3. What does Keoki ask for in 1819? Missionaries to bring Christianity.
4. What must Abner Hale do before he can be sent as a missionary to Hawaii? Get a wife.
5. How old is Jerusha? 22.
6. Who is she in love with? Capt. Hoxworth.
7. Why do the Bromley's think Jerusha will be interested in marrying Hale? She is love-sick and too old to not be married..
8. What happens to Jerusha's letters from Capt. Hoxworth? Her father hides them.
9. How does Hale react when Jerusha tells him about Capt. Hoxworth? Says he will leave in the morning. She will find a handsome husband.
10. Why does Hale hit Jerusha on the ship? She is begging to die.
11. Who does Keoki swim out to meet from the ship? His parents—Queen Malama and Kelolo.
12. To whom is Malama married? Her brother Kelolo.
13. Who is Noelani? Girl given to Hale and Jerusha by Queen Malama.
14. Why does Jerusha faint when she is teaching Queen Malama? Pregnant.
15. Why does Jerusha rescue the Hawaiian baby? Was to be killed for having a birthmark.

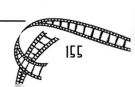

HAWAII VIEWING GUIDE—TEACHER PAGE 2

16. Whom do the sailors try to kidnap? Who saves her? Keoki's sister. Hale.

17. Who is the captain of the visiting ship? How does he react when he sees Jerusha? Capt. Hoxworth. Says he loves her and left her a virgin.

18. Why does Hale ask Queen Malama for land? Build a church.

19. According to Keoki, how many kinds of adultery are there? Give some examples. 22—mother/son, wife of brother, wife of friend, etc.

20. Why does Abner refuse the help of the midwives? Was this a wise decision? Explain. Won't submit her to heathens. Yes, the number one midwife would have killed the baby and number two midwife would have pulled the baby out..

21. Who is the first member of Hale's church? Llike.

22. What are some of the rules which Malama's new law decrees? No adultry. Women can't swim out to the boats. No sailors after dark.

23. Who sets the church on fire? Why? Sailors. Can't stay after dark.

24. Whom does Hoxworth take with him when he leaves? Llike.

25. What news does Jerusha's letter bring? Her sister died.

26. Why is Abraham Hulet banned from the church? Married a Hawaiian woman.

27. What teaching by Keoki angers Hale? Teaches about myths.

28. Why won't Hale make Keoki a preacher? He's not white.

29. Why does Malama call for Hale and Jerusha when she dies? Become a Christian.

30. What causes the wind to start? Death of Queen Malama.

31. What does Kololo do to himself after Malama dies? Puts out teeth and bangs head.

32. What happens to Malama's bones? Taken to Bora Bora.

33. What happens to Keoki's baby? Why? Drowned by Keoki. Deformed.

34. Why aren't Hawaiians used as slaves? Too few of them.

35. Why is measles so deadly to the Hawaiians? They have no resistance.

36. Who dies at the beach? Keoki.

37. What does Hoxworth bring Jerusha as a gift? A house.

38. Why can't Hale accept the gift? How does Hoxworth react? She died. He hits Hale.

39. Where does Hale send his children? Why? Grandparent in Boston.

40. Who offers to help Hale continue his work? Man who was birth-defect baby.

Name _____

HAWAII TEST

Matching

1. Rafer Hoxworth   A. Carries Malami's bones back to Bora Bora

2. Rev. John Whipple   B. Servant girl given to Hale and Jerusha

3. Abner Hale   C. Says he loves his wife more than God

4. Keoki   D. Banished from the church for marrying a Hawaiian

5. Queen Malama   E. Gives birth to a deformed baby

6. Noelani   F. Performs a marriage not sanctioned by the church

7. Lliki   G. Writes a letter to the British king

8. Jerusha   H. Has three children

9. Kelolo   I. Wants to be a Hawaiian minister

10. Abraham Hewlett   J. Brings a house to Hawaii for Herusha

True or False

_____ 1. Jerusha's letters from Hoxworth never arrived.

_____ 2. Hale dated Jerusha for a year before marriage.

_____ 3. Jerusha begs to die on the ship because she is so ill.

_____ 4. Keoki kneels before his mother for respect.

_____ 5. Kelolo is Malama's brother and husband.

_____ 6. The Hawaiians valued all human life.

_____ 7. Hawaiians recognized twenty kinds of adultery.

_____ 8. The midwives help deliver Jerusha's baby.

_____ 9. The first member of Hale's church is Keoki.

_____ 10. Malalma makes a law that girls cannot swim out to the ships.

_____ 11. Keoki dies when trying to put out the church fire.

_____ 12. Hale lives in Jerusha's house from Hoxworth.

_____ 13. Keoki teaches the children old Hawaiian chants about their migration to Hawaii.

_____ 14. Half of the Hawaiian population dies from measles.

_____ 15. The grown baby with the birthmark offers to help Hale in his ministry.

HAWAII TEST PAGE 2

Discussion: Answer in complete sentences:

1. Can a missionary movement truly respect the native culture? Explain.

2. Jerusha says to Hale, "I don't believe in your God of wrath . . . I've never seen a people more generous, more loving, more filled with Christian sweetness than these. I will not believe God has rejected them simply because they have not been baptized. You will stay here and shelter and protect these people. You will win them to a merciful God with bonds of charity so strong, they'll belong to Him forever . . . by offering what you've valued most and found it hardest go give—to them and me—your love." He then embraces her. What role does this scene play in the film? Explain.

3. Read the article about early Hawaiian history found at http://www.workersforjesus.com/hawaiians.htm. Underline or highlite accurate historical information portrayed in the movie. Explain at least three of the items which you chose.

HAWAII TEST ANSWER KEY

1. J
2. F
3. C
4. I
5. G
6. E
7. B
8. H
9. A
10. D
11. False
12. False
13. True
14. True
15. True
16. False
17. True
18. False
19. False
20. True
21. False
22. False
23. True
24. False
25. True
26. Answers will vary. If a missionary accepts the culture's religion, he negates the spread of Christianity. If he objects, he alienates the new population.
27. Hale softens in his treatment of the Hawaiians. He begins to take part in politics and tries to help them through the church. He stays to make a difference.

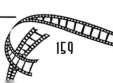

chapter 12

The Whole Truth

Research Project on a Historical Movie

OBJECTIVES

- Students will research the validity of a historical movie using internet sources.
- Students will write a three page typed research paper using MLA documentation.

NOTES TO THE TEACHER

This project should be mentioned at least three weeks prior to the actual assignment. You should give students two to three weeks to complete the entire project.

POSSIBLE PROBLEMS

Since the movies are to viewed outside of school, you should get parental permission for the students' movie choices to eliminate any possible problems.

PROCEDURES

1. **Permission Letter for History/Movie Project**—Send this letter home to parents/guardians to insure their cooperation and understanding of the assignment.

2. **Historical Movie Project**—This handout gives specific requirements for the project.

3. **Historical Movies Idea List**—This list may help students to see what kinds of movies would be appropriate for research.

4. **Basic Forms for Electronic Sources**—This information sheet will guide students in citing sources in the body of the paper and writing the Works Cited page.

5. **History Movie Paper Rubric**—Use this rubric to assign grades to students' papers.

Name _____

PERMISSION LETTER FOR HISTORY/MOVIE PROJECT

Dear Parents or Guardian,

During the week of _____, your student is to view a historical movie outside of class and then write a research paper exploring the validity of the movie's presentation of the historical content. The finished research paper is due _____.

I need you to help your student select a historical movie to view. Because the movie is to be viewed outside of class, I need parent approval for the choice. The rating of the movie doesn't matter so long as the parent/guardian approves.

Thanks for your help,

Film Teacher

_____has my permission to watch
(student name)

_____ for his/her historical movie research project and then
(title)

research the validity of the information presented in the movie. I understand that the research paper is worth

140 points and can significantly affect my student's grade in the class.

_____   _____

(parent or guardian)   (date)

Name _____

HISTORICAL MOVIE PROJECT

1. Choose a historical movie to watch on your own or in groups outside of class.

2. Research the validity of the movie.

3. Write a three-page typed paper about the validity of the movie.

Paper Requirements

1. Paper must use at least three sources. All may be internet sources. You must turn in **printed copies of your sources**.

2. The paper must be typed in a 12 point font and double-spaced.

3. Cite sources within the paper using MLA format. Include a Works Cited page at the end of the paper.

4. Paper must have an **introduction** which identifies the title of the movie, the year the movie came out, and the director of the movie. Be sure you have a clear thesis.

5. The **body** of the paper may include a brief summary of the movie. You may give some actual history of the time period or event depicted in the movie. You must then examine the validity of historical events in the movie. Be sure to give sources for quotes, paraphrased material, statistics, etc. Do not use citations for summary and your personal opinion.

6. You must cite a source in the text in order to put it on the Works Cited page.

7. The paper should have a **conclusion** which summarizes the paper.

8. **Works Cited** page should list all sources used in alphabetical order.

REEL WRITING

Name _____

HISTORICAL MOVIES IDEA LIST

Here is a list of possible movies to use for the historical movie project. The list is only a beginning. There are many more possible movies which could be added to the list.

1. *Black Hawk Down*
2. *Pearl Harbor*
3. *We Were Soldiers*
4. *Titanic*
5. *The Aviator*
6. *Apollo 13*
7. *The Patriot*
8. *Brave Heart*
9. *The Alamo*
10. *The Longest Day*
11. *Gettysburg*
12. *Band of Brothers*
13. *Saving Private Ryan*
14. *A Bridge Too Far*
15. *Hotel Rwanda*
16. *The Memphis Belle*
17. *Pork Chop Hill*
18. *Separate But Equal*
19. *Spartacus*
20. *Elizabeth*

21. *Master and commander*
22. *Sergeant York*
23. *Chicago*
24. *Patton*
25. *Tora, Tora, Tora*
26. *Platoon*
27. *Apocalypse Now*
28. *Born on the Fourth of July*
29. *Full Metal Jacket*
30. *Casualties of War*
31. *Mash*
32. *The Graduate*
33. *Christopher Columbus*
34. *Ben Hur*
35. *Gladiator*
36. *Amadeus*
37. *Shakespeare in Love*
38. *Gone with the Wind*
39. *Schindler's List*
40. *Forest Gump*

Name _____

BASIC FORMS FOR ELECTRONIC SOURCES

The MLA Style Manual provides extensive examples of electronic source citations. If your particular case is not covered here, consult the *MLA Handbook*.

If no author is given for a web page or electronic source, start with and alphabetize by the title of the piece and use a shortened version of the title for parenthetical citations.

A Web site

Author(s). "Name of Page." Date of Posting/Revision. <u>Name of institution/organization affiliated with the site</u>. Date of Access <electronic address>.

It is necessary to list your date of access because web postings are often updated, and information available at one date may no longer be available later. Be sure to include the complete address for the site. Also, note the use of angled brackets around the electronic address; MLA requires them for clarity.

Web site examples

Beaver, Jim. "Hawaii." 20 Dec. 2005. <u>Internet Movie Data Base</u>. 20 Dec. 2005 <http://www.imdb.com/title/tt0060491/>.
"Project Gutenberg." 2005. <u>Project Gutenberg Organization</u>. 20 Dec. 2005 <http://www.gutenberg.org/>.

An article on a web site

It is necessary to list your date of access because web postings are often updated, and information available at one date may no longer be available later. Be sure to include the <u>complete</u> address for the site. Also, note the use of angled brackets around the electronic address; MLA requires them for clarity.

Author(s)."Article Title." <u>Name of web site</u>. Date of posting/revision. Name of institution/organization affiliated with site. Date of access <electronic address>.

Article on a web site

Porter, Michael. "Movies That Teach Values." <u>The Cutting Edge</u>. 15 Dec. 1999. Television Classroom. 16 Jan. 2005 <http://www.cuttingedge.com>.

Griffin, Stan. "The Hawaiians." <u>Workers for Jesus</u>. 20 Dec. 2005 <http://wwwlworkersforjesus.com/hawaiians.htm>.

"General Information about Hawaiian Shield Volcanoes." <u>Hawaii Center for Volcanology</u>. 4 Apr. 2005. Hawaii Education. 23 Jan. 2006<http://www.soest.hawaii.ed/GG/FCV/haw_volc.html>.

An article in an online journal or magazine

Author(s). "Title of Article." <u>Title of Journal</u> Volume. Issue (Year): Pages/Paragraphs. Date of Access <electronic address>.

Some electronic journals and magazines provide paragraph or page numbers; include them if available. This format is also appropriate to online magazines; as with a print version, you should provide a complete publication date rather than volume and issue number.

Name _____

BASIC FORMS FOR ELECTRONIC SOURCES PAGE 2

Online journal article

Young, Mark. "Finding Values in Movies." <u>Our Past in Video</u> 5.8 (2001): 58 pgs. 5 Jan. 2000 <http://www.videopast.org.htm>.

Your Works Cited List

The works cited list should appear at the end of your essay. It provides the information necessary for a reader to locate and be able to read any sources you cite in the essay. **Each source you cite in the essay must appear in your works-cited list; likewise, each entry in the works-cited list must be cited in your text.** Preparing your works cited list using MLA style is covered in the *MLA Style Manual*. Here are some guidelines for preparing your works cited list.

List Format

- Begin your works cited list on a separate page from the text of the essay under the label Works Cited (with no quotation marks, underlining, etc.), which should be centered at the top of the page.
- Make the first line of each entry in your list flush left with the margin. Subsequent lines in each entry should be indented one-half inch. This is known as a **hanging indent.**
- **Double-space** all entries, with no skipped spaces between entries.
- Keep in mind that <u>**underlining**</u> and *italics* are equivalent; never use both.
- **Alphabetize** the list of works cited by the **first word** in each entry (usually the author's last name).

Basic Rules for Citations

- **Authors' names are inverted** (last name first); if a work has more than one author, invert only the first author's name, follow it with a comma, then continue listing the rest of the authors.
- If you have cited more than one work by a particular author, order them alphabetically by title, and use three hyphens in place of the author's name for every entry after the first.
- When an author appears both as the sole author of a text and as the first author of a group, list solo-author entries first.
- If **no author is given** for a particular work, **alphabetize by the title** of the piece and **use a shortened version of the title for parenthetical citations.**
- Capitalize each word in the titles of articles, books, etc. This rule does not apply to articles, short prepositions, or conjunctions unless one is the first word of the title or subtitle.
- **Underline or italicize titles of books, journals, magazines, newspapers, and films.**
- **Use quotation marks around the titles of articles in journals, magazines, and newspapers.** Also use quotation marks for the titles of short stories, book chapters, poems, and songs.
- List page numbers efficiently, when needed. If you refer to a journal article that appeared on pages 225 through 250, list the page numbers on your Works Cited page as 225-50.

Name _____

BASIC FORMS FOR ELECTRONIC SOURCES PAGE 3

Parenthetical Documentation Within Body of Paper

- You must document **direct quotations, paraphrased material, and statistics**.
- You **do not have to document common knowledge** such as **widely accepted facts, widely known proverbs, and simple definitions**. If you find the same information is three or more sources, you may consider it common knowledge. If you are in doubt, go ahead and document it.
- Do your works cited list first. **Whatever is listed first** in the works cited list will be used for the parenthetical documentation.
- A parenthetical documentation is **in parenthesis followed by the end punctuation** of the sentence it follows. It includes the **author's last name or a shortened title and the page reference if one is given**. For internet sources, there may not be a page number.

Examples:

- "Videos are one of the most effective methods of teaching values" (Porter).
- The early Hawaiians believed that nature required human sacrifice ("Gods").
- One fourth of the Hawaiian population was killed from measles (Griffin 3).
- The Hawaiian Islands may include as many as 130 islands in the Archipelago ("Shield Volcanoes").

REEL WRITING

Name _____

HISTORY MOVIE PAPER RUBRIC

	Weak (4 pts.)	**A**verage (6 pts.)	**G**ood (8 pts.)	**E**xcellent (10 pts.)
Appearance Double-spaced				
Introduction And Thesis				
Organization				
Supporting Details				
Internal Documentation				
Proof Validity or Lack of Validity				
Conclusion (Thesis, summary, clincher)				
Sentence Structure (Run-ons, fragments)				

Spelling (10 points, five points off for each error)_____

Grammar, punctuation, word choice, other (10 points)_____

Works Cited page (three sources, form, 10 points)_____

Source copies included (three, 30 points)_____   **Total Points:**_____/140

chapter 13
Tuning In
Radio: Accepting Others

OBJECTIVES

- Students will simulate disabilities and write personal reactions to the exercises.
- Students will learn some of the history of the inclusion movement.
- Students will write a five paragraph essay about learning from disabled persons.

NOTES TO THE TEACHER

Radio is a movie about an African American male in Anderson, South Carolina, in 1876. Coach Jones and his football team adopt the young man as a sort of mascot-water boy. He gets nicknamed Radio because he loves radios and likes to work on them. Under the tutorage of Coach Jones, Radio thrives. His speech gets clearer and his social skills get refined. In the process, the community learns to accept people with disabilities like Radio.

Radio is rated PG and is 109 minutes long.

POSSIBLE PROBLEMS

None.

PROCEDURES

1. **Rosa Parks**—Make a transparency and then turn the transparency over to make a copy on which the writing appears backwards like a mirror image. Have students read the article and answer questions. This simulates reading processing disabilities.

2. **Disability Exercises**—Students do a variety of experiments to simulate different kinds of disabilities.

3. **Reaction Paper**—Students share reactions to the disability exercises.

4. *Radio* **Viewing Guide**—Students answer these questions as they watch the movie.

5. *Radio* **Essay**—Students write a five paragraph essay after viewing the movie.

6. *Radio* **Essay Rubric**—Use this rubric to assign grades to students' essays.

Print this paper on a transparency sheet. Then turn is backwards on the copy machine to make a copy where the writing is inverted like a mirror image. Run off a set of papers for students to use to read and answer questions. The exercise will give students an idea what it would be like to have a reading processing disability.

ROSA PARKS

Rosa Parks is an African-American woman who became famous for instigating the Montgomery Alabama bus boycott December 1, 1955. Mrs. Parks was already seated when a white bus rider boarded the bus and demanded to take her seat. She refused to stand and was, subsequently, arrested. She was the first African-American to be arrested for this crime.

Dr. Martin Luther King, Jr., was pastor of the Dexter Avenue Baptist Church in Montgomery. He and other members of the community felt a protest of some kind was warranted. A bus boycott was organized by Dr. King and the African-American community which lasted for more than a year.

The boycott finally ended when the United States Supreme Court declared on November 13, 1956, that Alabama's state and local laws establishing segregation on buses were illegal.

Rosa Parks died on October 24, 2005 at the age of 92. She will long be remembered for her part in the civil rights movement.

Answer these questions about the article:

1. Why was Rosa Parks arrested?
2. Who organized the bus boycott?
3. How long did the boycott last?
4. What brought about the end of the boycott?
5. When did Rosa Parks die? How old was she?

DISABILITY EXERCISES

You will do a variety of experiments with your students to make them simulate being disabled.

1. Do the Rosa Parks story to show them what a reading processing disability would be like. Print this story on a transparency sheet. Then turn the sheet backwards on the copy machine to make a copy on which the writing is inverted like a mirror image. Run off a set of papers for students to use to read and answer questions. The exercise will give students an idea of what it would be like to have a reading processing disability.

2. Ask students to write something with the wrong hand.

3. Divide the class into teams. Give each team a pair of rubber gloves and a paper cup filled with twenty pennies. Each person must pour the coins out on a desk and then pick them up wearing the gloves. Then the next person puts on the gloves and performs the tack. The first team to finish wins.

4. Use clothesline cut into lengths to bind students' arms or legs together. The line should be tied tightly around the arms and body just above the elbows. Or the line for the feet should be tied in a circle a little bigger than the ankles and then the feet are put through to the ankles to restrict walking. The line forms a kind of circle sling which the feet are placed through to the ankles.

5. Students place cotton in their ears to simulate deafness.

6. Students tape wax paper over their eyes to simulate sight problems.

Have each student adopt at least two disabilities and then try to perform simple tasks. Here are some suggestions:

1. Walk around the school trying to keep up with the class.
2. Try dribbling a ball.
3. Try jump roping.
4. Try playing Red Rover.

Reaction Paper

Describe your reaction to each of the following tasks. What did you learn about yourself?

1. Writing name with wrong hand

2. Reading backwards writing

3. Gloved hand relay

4. What disabilities did you "adopt"? How did you feel as a result of the disabilities? What adjustments did you have to make? Were you able to do simple tasks such as walking, jumping rope, dribbling a ball, playing Red Rover? Explain.

 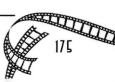

Name _____

RADIO VIEWING GUIDE

Briefly identify these characters as you watch the movie:

1. Cuba Gooding Jr. ....James Kennedy/Radio—

2. Ed Harris .... Coach Jones—

3. Alfre Woodard .... Principal Daniels—

4. S. Epatha Merkerson .... Maggie—

5. Brent Sexton .... Honeycutt—

6. Debra Winger ... Linda.—

7. Sarah Drew .... Mary Helen—

8. Chris Mulkey .... Frank Clay—

9. Riley Smith .... Johnny Clay—

Discussion questions: Answer these questions after you watch the movie. Use complete sentences.

1. When and where does the film open?

2. Why do you think the boys bind Radio and lock him up in a shed? Are they evil or just acting on influences around them?

3. Why does Coach Jones want to help Radio so much? In what ways does his relationship with Radio affect his relationship with his own daughter?

4. Principal Daniels is something of a champion of disabled students' rights. Explain.

REEL WRITING

Name _____

RADIO VIEWING GUIDE PAGE 2

5. Is Frank Clay the "bad guy" of the movie? Why does he act the way he does?

6. The barber shop seems to be the public forum for the town. Explain.

7. What prejudices cause the policeman to distrust Radio?

8. Explain how Radio gets his nickname.

9. Why does Coach Jones give up his job as head coach? Do you agree with his decision? Explain.

10. Does the "real life" Radio look as you had imagined? Do you think the director did a good job of casting the part of Radio to Cuba Gooding, Jr.? Explain.

Name _____

RADIO ESSAY

You will write an in-class essay about the film *Radio*.
Requirements:

1. Introduction which includes the title of the film and introduces the thesis statement.

2. Thesis statement at the end of the introduction. It should echo the quote by Coach Jones: "We weren't teaching Radio; Radio was teaching us."

3. Three body paragraphs which prove the thesis. You may include summary of incidents from the film to prove each point.

4. Conclusion which re-states the thesis and summarizes the body paragraphs.

5. Use correct spelling, grammar, sentence structure, and word choice.

6. Use present tense.

7. Do not use second person pronouns (you, your, etc.).

8. Length should be 1–3 handwritten pages.

REEL WRITING

Name _____

RADIO ESSAY RUBRIC

	Weak (4 pts.)	**A**verage (6 pts.)	**G**ood (8 pts.)	**E**xcellent (10 pts.)
Appearance				
Introduction (development and strategy)				
Clear Thesis				
Body I (Topic sentence, developed)				
Body II (Topic sentence, developed)				
Body III (Topic sentence, developed)				
Conclusion (Thesis, summary, clincher)				
Sentence structure (Run-ons, fragments)				

Spelling (10 points, five points off for each error)_____

Grammar, punctuation, word choice, other (10 points)_____

Total Points:_____/100

chapter 14

Next Category, Please

Never Been Kissed:
Stereotypes

OBJECTIVES

- Students will be able to define stereotype, flat character, round character, static character, and dramatic character.
- Students will identify television stereotypes and create posters.
- Students will devise plans to eliminate cliques in their school.
- Students will practice public speaking skills.

NOTES TO THE TEACHER

Never Been Kissed is a movie about Josie Geller, a reporter who must go back to high school and pose as a high school student to get a story. She relives her past high school experience at first and then discovers the secrets of popularity. The stereotyped groups in the movie are typical of most American high schools.

Never Been Kissed is rated PG 13 for sex related material and some drug content and is 108 minutes long.

POSSIBLE PROBLEMS

Be sure to preview the film. You might want to skip the scenes which include Josie's best friend Anita. In scene 2, the friend talks crudely about her love life. The scene starts when Josie closes the blinds in her office. In scene 18, Anita, the friend comes to the school and teaches a sex education class in which she has students put condoms on bananas. The scene starts with a view of a skeleton in a classroom. My students assured me the scenes were fine for their age group (they are so mature), but I skipped them anyway.

PROCEDURES

1. **Stereotype Definitions**—Use this transparency to give definitions to students.

2. **Television Stereotypes**—Students create posters of traditional television stereotypes and present to the class.

3. *Never Been Kissed* **Viewing Guide**—Students answer these questions as they watch the movie.

4. **School Stereotype Group Activity**—Students make a plan to eliminate cliques at their school and present the plans to the class.

STEREOTYPE DEFINITIONS

Stereotyping—Using labels or categories to describe others. These labels may be based on such characteristics as clothing, looks, speech, actions, or group association.

Flat Character—A character with only one or two developed characteristics. He will be a minor character in a story.

Round Character—A character with three or more developed characteristics. This character is three dimensional. He will be a prominent character in a story.

Static Character—A character in a story who doesn't change in a significant way.

Dramatic Character—A character in a story who changes in a significant way. This character will usually be a main character who learns a lesson or matures in some way.

- Some stereotype characters are necessary in a story. Most static and flat characters are stereotypes.

- Stereotypes can be helpful to characterize minor characters quickly in a story.

- Most round or dramatic characters are not stereotypes.

- Stereotypes can be dangerous when they present groups in a negative way.

Name _____

TELEVISION STEREOTYPES

Stereotypes are used in television programs because they enable a viewer to understand a character's role quickly and easily. A half hour show doesn't allow enough time to develop well-rounded characters. Stereotypes are used as sort of stock characters which are easily understood by the audience.

You will be divided into groups of four and assigned a television stereotype. You are to create a "Wanted" poster for your stereotype. You will need a piece of poster board and markers.

Requirements:

- Explain why this person is wanted.
- Explain how this person behaves.
- Explain how this person looks.
- List places where this person might be found.
- Draw a picture of this person on your poster.

Stereotypes:

1. Grandmother
2. Bully
3. Cop
4. Model
5. Doctor
6. Lawyer
7. Drug Pusher
8. Nerd
9. Teenager
10. Scientist
11. Detective
12. Burglar
13. Blonde Female
14. Cowboy
15. Doctor

REEL WRITING

Name _____

NEVER BEEN KISSED VIEWING GUIDE

Briefly Identify each character as you watch the movie:

1. Drew Barrymore .... Josie Geller—

2. Michael Vartan .... Sam Coulson—

3. David Arquette .... Rob Gellar—

4. Jeremy Jordan .... Guy Perkins—

5. Molly Shannon .... Anita Olesky—

6. John C. Reilly .... Gus Strauss—

Answer these questions as you watch the movie:

1. What is Josie's job?

Fast forward through scene 2—Begins when Josie closes the blinds and Anita, her friend, comes into the office.

2. What kind of kiss does Josie want?

3. What is Josie's assignment?

4. What does Josie want to borrow from her brother Rob?

5. Where does Rob work?

6. What was Josie's high school name?

7. Why does Josie have to wear a Mexican hat?

8. What does "pastoral" mean?

9. Who takes Josie's car?

10. What club does Josie join?

11. Where does Josie find her car?

12. What does Mr. Coulson say is the advantage of being in disguise?

13. What is the prom theme?

14. What does Rob say it takes to be popular?

15. Where is Josie's camera?

16. The guy says the brownie has vitamins and THC. What does that mean?

17. Why is everyone calling Josie a loser when she enters school?

18. What does Billy, her prom date, do to her?

19. How does Rob get popular so quickly?

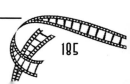

Name _____

NEVER BEEN KISSED VIEWING GUIDE PAGE 2

Skip Scene 18. It begins when the camera shows a skeleton in a classroom. The new prom theme is "Meant for Each Other: Famous Couples Throughout History."

20. How much time does Josie have to complete her story?

21. Who asks Josie to prom?

22. Who dresses like Barbies?

23. What do the nerd kids dress as for the prom?

24. Who gets awarded Prom King? Prom Queen?

25. What happens to the dog food?

26. What high school groups still remain at the school?

27. If the teacher accepts her apology, what must he do?

28. Why does Sam apologize?

29. Who is the new assistant coach?

30. What had Rob wanted to do after high school?

Teacher

NEVER BEEN KISSED VIEWING GUIDE—TEACHER

Briefly Identify each character as you watch the movie:

1. Drew Barrymore .... Josie Geller—

2. Michael Vartan .... Sam Coulson—

3. David Arquette .... Rob Gellar—

4. Jeremy Jordan .... Guy Perkins—

5. Molly Shannon .... Anita Olesky—

6. John C. Reilly .... Gus Strauss—

Answer these questions as you watch the movie:

1. What is Josie's job? Copy editor.

Fast forward through scene 2—Begins when Josie closes the blinds and Anita, her friend, comes into the office.

2. What kind of kiss does Josie want? A kiss that makes everything hazy from the person you will spend the rest of your life with.

3. What is Josie's assignment? Go back to high school.

4. What does Josie want to borrow from her brother Rob? His car.

5. Where does Rob work? Packing store.

6. What was Josie's high school name? Josie Groosie.

7. Why does Josie have to wear a Mexican hat? Tardy.

8. What does "pastoral" mean? In the country.

9. Who takes Josie's car? Guy Perkins and his friends.

10. What club does Josie join? Denominators.

11. Where does Josie find her car? Football field.

12. What does Mr. Coulson say is the advantage of being in disguise? We are free to be what we want.

13. What is the prom theme? Millennium.

14. What does Rob say it takes to be popular? One person to think you are cool.

15. Where is Josie's camera? Pin on sweater.

16. The guy says the brownie has vitamins and THC. What does that mean? Marijuana.

17. Why is everyone calling Josie a loser when she enters school? It's stamped on her head.

18. What does Billy, her prom date, do to her? Throws eggs.

19. How does Rob get popular so quickly? Wins a cold slaw eating contest.

NEVER BEEN KISSED VIEWING GUIDE—TEACHER PAGE 2

Skip Scene 18. It begins when the camera shows a skeleton in a classroom. The new prom theme is "Meant for Each Other: Famous Couples Throughout History."

20. How much time does Josie have to complete her story? Two weeks.

21. Who asks Josie to prom? Guy.

22. Who dresses like Barbies? The three popular girls.

23. What do the nerd kids dress as for the prom? DNA.

24. Who gets awarded Prom King? Prom Queen? Guy and Josie.

25. What happens to the dog food? Falls on the Barbie girls.

26. What high school groups still remain at the school? Beautiful girls, the smart kids, the perfect guy.

27. If the teacher accepts her apology, what must he do? Kiss her on the pitcher's mound.

28. Why does Sam apologize? He's late.

29. Who is the new assistant coach? Rob.

30. What had Rob wanted to do after high school? Play professional baseball.

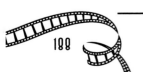

Name _____

SCHOOL STEREOTYPE GROUP ACTIVITY

After you watch the movie, you will be divided into groups of four. In each group, you are to identify at least six cliques in your school and determine the characteristics of each. Then you are to formulate a plan with at least four steps to help eliminate the cliques.

Each group will present its plan to the class.

If possible, plans should be put into action.

OBJECTIVES

- Students will practice public speaking.
- Students will recognize common elements in traditional fairy tales.
- Students will write revised versions of traditional fairy tales.
- Students will practice reading aloud.

NOTES TO THE TEACHER

Ever After is a revised version of the Cinderella story. Danielle is left with her stepmother and stepsisters after the death of her father. She is friends with the artists Leonardo da Vinci and Gustave. They help her gain an audience with the Prince to beg the release of a favorite servant. When the Prince is attracted to her, the conflicts begin.

Ever After is rated PG 13 and is 121 minutes long.

POSSIBLE PROBLEMS

None

PROCEDURES

1. **Group Improvisation Fairy Tales**—Students perform traditional fairy tales and brainstorm a list of common elements in fairy tales.

2. *Ever After* **Viewing Guide**—Students answer questions as they watch the move.

3. **Read aloud examples of revised fairy tales**—The teacher should obtain books which contain revised versions of fairy tales and read several aloud. Possible sources might include *Factured Fairy Tales* by A.J. Jacobs, *12 Fabulously Funny Fairy Tale Plays* by Justin McCory Martin, and *Politically Correct Bedtime Stories: Modern Tales for Our Life and Times* by James Finn Garner.

4. **Revised Fairy Tale and Rubric**—Students are to write a new version of a traditional fairy tale. Have students read the stories aloud. Use the rubric to assign grades to students' stories.

Name _____

GROUP IMPROVISATION FAIRY TALES

You will be divided into groups of four students. Each group will be assigned a traditional fairy tale.

You will talk about the fairy tale and read it if necessary (find fairytales online).

Each person in the group will become a character. You may also use a narrator.

You will perform the fairy tale for the class as an improvisation.

Possible Fairytales:

- The Three Little Pigs
- Little Red Riding Hood
- The Three Bears
- Snow White
- Sleeping Beauty
- Jack and the Beanstalk
- Rumplesteilskin
- The Princess and the Pea
- Rapunzel
- The Ugly Duckling
- The Red Hen
- The Tortoise and the Hare

After you view the improvisations, come up with a list of common elements in fairy tales.

Name _____

EVER AFTER VIEWING GUIDE

Briefly identify each character as you watch the movie:

1. Drew Barrymore .... Danielle De Barbarac—

2. Anjelica Huston .... Baroness Rodmilla De Ghent—

3. Dougray Scott .... Prince Henry—

4. Patrick Godfrey .... Leonardo da Vinci—

5. Megan Dodds .... Marguerite De Ghent—

6. Melanie Lynskey .... Jacqueline De Ghent—

7. Timothy West .... King Francis—

8. Judy Parfitt .... Queen Marie—

9. Lee Ingleby .... Gustave—

Discussion questions: Answer these questions in complete sentences after you watch the movie:

1. List at least six similarities between *Ever After* and the traditional Cinderella fairy tale.

2. Describe the character Marguerite. Is she a person in her own right or merely a product of her mother's own creation? Explain.

3. Which stepsister is sympathetic to Danielle? How does her relationship with her own mother influence her to be sympathetic?

4. What events have caused Danielle to champion the cause of equal rights for the poor?

5. Describe an instance in which Jacqueline is used for comic relief.

REEL WRITING

Name _____

EVER AFTER VIEWING GUIDE   PAGE 2

6. The stereotype of the "wicked stepmother" comes primarily from fairy tales. Is the stepmother truly wicked, or can you offer other reasons for her actions? Explain.

7. Which character plays the part of the fairy godmother in *Ever After*? Why is he a good choice for this role? Cite at least three times he performs magic for Danielle.

8. When the stepmother and Marguerite are called before the King and Queen, Danielle offers to speak for them. What request does she make on their behalf? Explain the irony of the result of her request.

9. List at least six differences between *Ever After* and the traditional fairy tale.

10. Do you think *Ever After* does a good job of making the Cinderella fairytale believable? Explain by giving specific examples from the movie.

Name _____

REVISED FAIRY TALE ASSIGNMENT AND RUBRIC

You are to take a traditional fairy tale and write a new version. The new story must be at least three neatly handwritten pages or two double-spaced typed pages in a 12 point font.

Your paper should be free of punctuation, spelling, grammar, word choice, and sentence structure errors.

	Weak (4 pts.)	**A**verage (6 pts.)	**G**ood (8 pts.)	**E**xcellent (10 pts.)
Appearance: **Neatness and length**				
Is the traditional story on which the new version is based clear?				
Are the descriptions of characters and setting vivid?				
Is the new version creative?				
Does the new version contain traditional fairy tale elements?				
Are the characters developed adequately?				
Does the story seem finished?				
Sentence structure (fragments or run-ons)				

Spelling (10 points, five points off for each error)_____

Grammar, punctuation, word choice, other (10 points)_____

Total Points:_____/100

chapter 16
The One That Got Away

Big Fish: Allusions

OBJECTIVES

- Students will analyze the symbolism of a poem.
- Students will recognize symbolism in a film.
- Students will be able to identify and explain allusions in literature.
- Students will write paragraphs which contain allusions.
- Students will gain public speaking practice.

NOTES TO THE TEACHER

Big Fish is a frame story. The outer story is about Will Bloom coming home to be with his father when he dies. Will hopes to really get to know his father beyond the wild stories his father has always told. The inner story is about Ed Bloom's life—the meeting of his wife, his life as a traveling salesman, and his encounters with many unique individuals. The film is filled with symbolism and allusions.

Big Fish is rated PG 13 and is 125 minutes long.

POSSIBLE PROBLEMS

None.

PROCEDURES

1. **"The Fish" by Elizabeth Bishop**—Students will find this poem at <http://bcs.bedfordstmartins.com/virtualit/poetry/fish_elements.html>. Read the poem together and discuss the meaning of the poem. The poem will have many parallels to *Big Fish*.

2. **Symbolism of Fish in Literature**—Use this transparency to help students determine symbolism of fish in literature.

3. *Big Fish* **Viewing Guide**—Students answer these questions as they watch the movie.

4. *Big Fish* **Discussion Questions and Allusions**—Allow students to answer these questions in groups and then share information with the entire class.

5. **Teacher Information Resources**—These web sites will help you understand the symbols and allusions in the film: <http://www.hollywoodjesus.com/big_fish.htm> <http://www.word-on-the-web.co.uk/films/bigfish.htm> <http://www.signonsandiego.com/uniontrib/20050812/news_1m12mcgrory.html>.

6. **Allusion Exercise**—Students write paragraphs which contain allusions to literature.

7. **Lagniappe**—Share this information with students about *Big Fish*.

8. **Fish Stories**—Make an outline of a fish on card stock and cut it out. Have students tell fish stories.

SYMBOLISM OF FISH IN LITERATURE

1. Fish are associated with Jesus in the Bible. He multiplies the loaves and the fishes to feed the five thousand and He makes his disciples into fishers of men.

2. Fish are associated with freedom because they must be caught to be controlled.

3. Fish may represent the spirit of man which is eternal in the sea of infinity.

4. Fish stories are exaggerated stories which get bigger and bigger each time they are told.

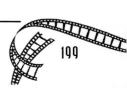

Name _____

BIG FISH VIEWING GUIDE

Briefly identify each character as you watch the movie:

1. Albert Finney .... Ed Bloom (Senior)—

2. Billy Crudup .... Will Bloom—

3. Jessica Lange .... Sandra Bloom (Senior)—

4. Helena Bonham Carter .... Jenny and the Witch—

5. Alison Lohman .... Sandra Bloom (Young)—

6. Matthew McGrory .... Karl the Giant—

7. David Denman .... Don Price (Age 18-22)—

8. Ada Tai .... Ping—

9. Arlene Tai .... Jing—

10. Danny DeVito—Amos Calloway—

Answer these questions as you watch the movie. Write down any reference you hear to "fish" or "water" as you watch this movie. A line will be provided for the references.

1. Why doesn't Will like his dad's stories?

2. How does Edward get his ring back from the fish?

3. Why does Will leave his rehearsal dinner angry?

4. What do the children see in the witch's eye?

_____

5. What happened to Edward to cause him to stay in bed three years?

6. What did he read while in bed?

7. Describe the giant.

8. How does he get Carl to leave the town?

9. What gift does the mayor give to Edward when he leaves?

_____

10. What problems does Edward encounter on the haunted road?

11. What does Jenny take from Edward? What does she do with them?

12. What form does the fish take in the lake?

13. How much older is Edward than Jenny?

Name _____

BIG FISH VIEWING GUIDE PAGE 2

14. What promise does Edward make to Jenny?

15. Why did time stop at the circus?

_____

16. What is the first clue Amos gives to Edward about the mystery woman?

17. What does Amos Calloway morph into?

18. What methods does Edward use to woo Sandra Templeton?

19. How does Don Price die?

_____

20. Why does Edward do dangerous missions in the war?

21. Why do the twins Jing and Ping help Ed escape the war?

22. What wrong message does Sandra Templeton receive about Ed during the war?

23. Why does Will tell his dad about an ice berg?

_____

24. What job does he take after the war?

25. How does Will find the adult Jenny?

26. According to Jenny, how did Edward "save" Spector?

27. Why does Jenny sell Edward her house after he vows to faithful to his wife?

28. Who is the "witch" in real life?

29. Who is Edward's "girl in the river"?

30. Explain how Will is able to tell the last story.

31. Which people show up in real life at the funeral?

Name _____

BIG FISH DISCUSSION QUESTIONS AND ALLUSIONS

Answer these questions in complete sentences after watching the movie. It may be helpful to answer these questions in groups.

1. What is Will and Edward's relationship like at the beginning of the movie? What has caused the division?.

2. At what point does Will accept his father just as he is?

3. Explain Will's last words: "That was my father's final joke, I guess. The man tells his stories so many times, he becomes the story. They live on after him, and in that way, he becomes immortal."

4. Why did the fish appear in the swimming pool when Will was cleaning it? What significance does the fish's appearance have in the last scene?

5. Explain the allusions of each of the following:

   • David and Goliath

   • Robert Frost's *The Road Not Taken*

   • Biblical time of testing

   • Garden of Eden

   • Jacob and Rachel

   • Moses

   • Baptism into death and resurrection

   • Redemption of mankind

   • Passing from life to death.

6. Explain how *Big Fish* is similar to Elizabeth Bishop's poem *The Fish*.

Teacher

BIG FISH VIEWING GUIDE—TEACHER

Answer these questions as you watch the movie. Write down any reference you hear to "fish" or "water" as you watch this movie. A line will be provided for the references.

1. Why doesn't Will like his dad's stories? Too long, too many times.

2. How does Edward get his ring back from the fish? Squeezes it out.

3. Why does Will leave his rehearsal dinner angry? His dad is telling the fish story again.

4. What do the children see in the witch's eye? How they will die.

   Wants water all the time.

5. What happened to Edward to cause him to stay in bed three years? He grew too fast for his muscles to and bones to keep up.

6. What did he read? Encyclopedia (all knowledge) to the "G's"—about goldfish.

7. Describe the giant. Hairy, tall, crooked head.

8. How does he get Carl to leave the town? Tells him to go to a town where there is more food.

9. What gift does the mayor give to Edward when he leaves? Key to the city.

   The biggest fish in the river gets that way by never being caught.

10. What problems does Edward encounter on the haunted road? Birds, bees, jumping spiders.

11. What does Jenny take from Edward? What does she do with them? Shoes—throws them over a clothesline—don't need protection in Spector.

12. What form does the fish take in the lake? Naked lady.

13. How much older is Edward than Jenny? Ten years.

14. What promise does Edward make to Jenny? He will return.

15. Why did time stop at the circus? He meets the love of his life.

    You're a big fish in a small pond. This is the ocean and you're drowning.

16. What is the first clue Amos gives to Edward about the mystery woman? She likes daffodils.

17. What does Amos Calloway morph into? Hell-hound, wild dog, werewolf.

18. What methods does Edward use to woo Sandra Templeton? Flowers, message on transparency, airplane message, field of daffodils.

19. How does Don Price die? Heart gave out.

    I've been thirsty my whole life.

20. Why does Edward do dangerous missions in the war? To reduce his time to get home early.

21. Why do the twins Jing and Ping help Ed escape the war? Tells about his true love.

22. What wrong message does Sandra Templeton receive about Ed during the war? Ed was killed.

23. Why does Will tell his dad about an ice berg? Father is hard to understand. 90% is under the surface.

    Ed: I was dried out. Sandra: I don't think I will ever dry out.

BIG FISH VIEWING GUIDE—TEACHER PAGE 2

24. What job does he take after the war? Traveling salesman.

25. How does Will find the adult Jenny? Deed of trust in his dad's papers.

26. According to Jenny, how did Edward "save" Spector? Bought the town and gave it .back

27. Why does Jenny sell Edward her house after he vows to faithful to his wife? She knows she can never catch him. Time to cut the line and let him go.

28. Who is the "witch" in real life? Jenny.

29. Who is Edward's "girl in the river"? His wife Sandra.

30. Explain how Will is able to tell the last story. He understands his father and is willing to start telling tells. He is giving up on "catching" his dad. He lets him go.

31. Which people show up in real life at the funeral? Twins, Karl, Jenny, poet, Mr. Calloway.

Discussion questions:

1. What is Will and Edward's relationship like at the beginning of the movie? What has caused the division? Doesn't know his father. Tired of the stories. Wants the truth.

2. At what point does Will accept his father just as he is? How do you know? He tells the story of his dad's death. He lets the "fish" go. He has accepted his dad and is willing to take over the role of storyteller.

3. Explain Will's last words: "That was my father's final joke, I guess. The man tells his stories so many times, he becomes the story. They live on after him, and in that way, he becomes immortal." Will is now telling his dad's stories. His dad is alive in the tall tales.

5. Explain the allusions of each of the following:

- David and Goliath—Ed gets Karl to leave the town.
- Robert Frost's *The Road Not Taken*—Ed takes the less traveled road through the forest while Karl takes the easy road.
- Biblical time of testing—Ed is attacked by a bird, bees, and jumping spiders.
- Garden of Eden—Spector—It is a perfect place where shoes (protection) are not needed.
- Jacob and Rachel—Biblical story in which Jacob must work seven years for Lebon to win Rachel in marriage. He is tricked the first time and must work seven more years. Ed must work for Mr. Calloway to get clues of his love's identity.

- Moses—Ed leads Ping and Jing out of their country to the promised land. Ed picks up a snake and it changes to a stick.
- Baptism into death and resurrection—Edward's car is underwater when he re-enters Spector. He dies and comes back to life.
- Redemption of mankind—Spector has fallen because of man's greed (sin nature). Ed buys the town for a price and then offers it back to the men as a free gift. All that is required is to receive the gift.
- Passing from life to death—Ed goes to the river and returns to immortality. He gives life to future generations through his stories.

6. Explain how *Big Fish* is similar to Elizabeth Bishop's poem *The Fish*. Will tries to "catch" his dad in the stories. His dad's health begins to fail. He lets his dad go when he begins the story of Ed's death. He releases the fish (his dad) and his dad becomes eternal.

Name _____

ALLUSION EXERCISE

An **allusion** is a reference to a famous person, place, thing, or part of another work of literature. It is assumed that the reader understands the allusion. The literary device stimulates ideas, associations, and extra information into the reader's mind with only a word or a phrase.

Here is an example:

- *After dropping out of college and running out of money, the prodigal son returned to his father.* (Luke 15:11-32)
- *Her brief mustard-seed idea germinated into a great business opportunity* (Matthew 17:20).
- Allusions in writing help the reader to visualize what is happening by creating a mental picture. But the reader must be aware of the allusion and must be familiar with what it refers to.
- Allusions are commonly made to the Bible, nursery rhymes, myths, famous fictional or historical characters or events, and Shakespeare. Allusions are often used in prose and poetry.

Here are some more examples:

- *My son is a real scrooge with his money.*
- The allusion to Scrooge should bring to mind someone who pinches pennies and does not like to spend money.
- *The mother demanded obedience, but when challenged, she had feet of clay.*
- This allusion refers to Daniel 2:31-45.
- *The young man wanted to impress his date, but an audition in the <u>Three Stooges</u> would have been more successful.*
- *The driving instructor chided his student for trying to be a Speedy Gonzales.*
- *When it was time to wake my baby, I placed a kiss on the cheek of my Sleeping Beauty.*

Here are some facts which you may be able to use to create your own allusions. Write at least four allusions to share with the class.

1. Brutus was the best friend who helped assassinate Julius Caesar.

2. Benedict Arnold was an American traitor.

3. Mother Teresa was a nun who devoted her entire life to caring for the poor and sick.

4. Kansas from the *Wizard of Oz* represents home.

5. Hamlet was a character who suffered an identity crisis.

6. Judas is the disciple who betrayed Jesus.

7. Robin Hood is famous for robbing from the rich and giving to the poor.

8. Napoleon was defeated at Waterloo.

9. Cinderella was forced to act as a servant to her wicked stepmother after her father died.

10. The Little Mermaid gave up the ocean world to be with the human she loved.

11. Hiroshima is the Japanese City on which the United States dropped an atomic bomb.

12. Gettysburg is the battle of the Civil War in which many soldiers were killed on both sides.

FISH LAGNIAPPE

Tim Burton has many allusions to other movies he directed in *Big Fish*.

1. Lures in the water in the opening scene—Look for the face of Jack Skellington's skull in the reflection of one of the lures on the left.

2. Ed Bloom's tie in the Daffodils scene—The tie has a picture of curling hill from *Nightmare Before Christmas.*

3. The breakfast device in the science fair project—This is the device which makes breakfast in *Pee-Wee's Great Adventure.*

4. The hand device which Edward Bloom sells—The device is reminiscent of the hands of Edward Scissorhands.

5. Hat worn by Amos Calloway at the circus—This is like the hat worn by Willy Wonka in the *Chocolate Factory.*

6. Ruby Slippers from Wizard of Oz—Look for the red boots hanging on the line at the entrance of Spector.

Name Symbolism:

1. Ed Bloom has *bloom-ed.* He has lived his life.

2. Will Bloom hasn't bloomed. When he begins to tell his father's stories he *will bloom.*

3. Diane Arbus is a photographer who likes to take pictures of freaks such as giants, witches, twins. Many of the images in Big Fish could reflect Arbus' work.

Name _____

FISH STORIES

You will create "fish stories" as a class. Remember that fish stories are exaggerated and often contain elements of magic, giants, fantastic events, etc.

The first person to receive the fish will tell the basic situation of the story. The basic situation introduces the characters, setting, and conflict. Then he will pass the fish to another person.

The second person will develop the conflicts of the story.

The third person will tell the climax of the story at least until the winner of the conflict is determined.

The fourth person will tell the resolution of the story and make the characters live happily ever after.

Then pass the fish to a new person and begin a new story.

chapter 17

Shiver Me Timbers!

Pirates of the Caribbean:
The Curse of the
Black Pearl: Jargon

OBJECTIVES

- Students will be able to define jargon and find examples of jargon in song lyrics.
- Students will write a song which contains pirate jargon.
- Students will practice public performance skills.

NOTES TO THE TEACHER

Pirates of the Caribbean is a fun movie filled with narrow escapes, special effects, and fight sequences. Elizabeth is kidnapped by the pirates from the *Black Pearl*. Will Tanner and Jack Sparrow go on a quest to rescue her. The movie has treasure, sword fights, skeletons, and revenge.

Pirates of the Caribbean is rated PG 13 and is 143 minutes long.

POSSIBLE PROBLEMS

The moonlight shows the pirates as skeletons. The images might scare young children but should be fine for high school students.

PROCEDURES

1. **Free Write**—Students write for ten minutes on the topic *Pirates* and then read aloud to the class.

2. ***Blow the Man Down***—Use this handout to teach the students a pirate song.

3. **Jargon**—Use this sheet to teach students the definition of jargon and to give them a pirate jargon list.

4. ***Pirates of the Caribbean* Viewing Guide**—Students answer these questions as they watch the movie.

5. **Group Pirate Song and Rubric**—Use this handout to get students to write pirate songs to perform for the class. Use the rubric to assign grades to students' performances.

Name _____

BLOW THE MAN DOWN

Oh, blow the man down, bullies, blow the man down!
Way, hey, blow the man down,
Oh, Blow the man down, bullies, blow him right down!
Oh, gimme some time to blow the man down.

As I was a-rollin' down Paradise Street,
Way, hey, blow the man down,
A big Irish copper I chanced for to meet,
Oh, gimme some time to blow the man down.

"Oh, you're a blackballer by the cut of your hair,
And you're a blackballer by the clothes that yez wear!"

Policeman, policeman, you do me great wrong,
I'm a flying-fish sailor just home from Hong Kong.

"No, you're signed on some packet that flies the black ball,
And you've robbed some poor Dutchman of boots, clothes, and all."

So, I smashed in his face and I stove in his jaw,
Sez he, "Look here, young fella, you're breakin' the law."

Well, they gave me six months in Liverpool town,
For a-beatin' and a-kickin' and a-blowin' him down.

A Liverpool ship and a Liverpool crew,
A Liverpool mate and a Scouse skipper, too.

We're Liverpool born, boys, and Liverpool bred,
Thick in the arm, boys, and thick in the head.

Name _____

JARGON

Jargon is language which is characteristic to a particular group. Jargon may be associated with sports, computer language, teacher terminology, medical terminology, citizen band radios, and **pirates**, etc.

Here are some examples of **Pirate Jargon**:

- Man overboard
- Strumpet
- Glass eye
- Popet
- Argh!
- Gar!
- Yo ho, ho!
- Polly want a cracker?
- Rum
- Treasure and treasure maps
- Walk the plank
- Shiver me timbers!
- Ahoy!
- Blimey!
- Blaggard
- Grub
- Gangway!
- Landlubber
- Me hearties
- Pieces of eight
- Lookout
- Anchor
- Ahoy
- Buccaneer
- Swashbuckler
- Grab thee a wench
- Matey
- "X" marks the spot
- Sea rover

Name _____

PIRATES OF THE CARIBBEAN VIEWING GUIDE

Briefly identify each character as you watch the movie:

1. Johnny Depp . . .Jack Sparrow—

2. Orlando Bloom . . . Will Turner—

3. Keira Knightley . . . Elizabeth Swann—

4. Jack Davenport . . . Commodore Norrington—

5. Jonathan Pryce . . . Governor Swann—

Answer the following questions as you watch the movie.

1. Why is Elizabeth Swan told not to sing about pirates?

2. What is the name of the boy who is rescued from the ocean? How does Elizabeth know he is a pirate?

3. What is the *Black Pearl*?

4. Why does Elizabeth fall over the wall into the water?

5. What is the pirate's real name?

6. Why does Sparrow enter the Blacksmith's shop?

7. Why do the pirates want to kidnap Elizabeth?

8. What does it mean to "demand parley"?

9. What does Elizabeth trade to get the pirates to leave?

10. Why does Jack Sparrow help Will get to the Black Pearl?

11. What was the nickname of Will's father?

12. Why are the men of the Black Pearl cursed?

13. What will end the curse?

14. What makes the crew look like skeletons?

15. Why is Anna Maria angry with Jack?

16. If Jack was the past captain of the *Black Pearl*, why didn't the curse fall on him?

17. Why does Jack want to kill Barbosa?

18. How does Jack say he escaped the island?

19. What did Jack use for a rope?

20. Why didn't the curse lift when the coin was thrown in?

21. What is the monkey's name?

22. How did Jack really get off the island?

Name _____

PIRATES OF THE CARIBBEAN VIEWING GUIDE PAGE 2

23. What does a ship symbolize to Jack?

24. What does Elizabeth promise the commodore if he saves Will?

25. What happens to the crew when the curse is lifted?

26. Who saves Jack's life from hanging? How?

27. Who is in control of the *Black Pearl* at the end of the movie?

REEL WRITING

Teacher

PIRATES OF THE CARIBBEAN VIEWING GUIDE—TEACHER ANSWERS

Briefly identify each character as you watch the movie:

1. Johnny Depp . . .Jack Sparrow—

2. Orlando Bloom . . . Will Turner—

3. Keira Knightley . . . Elizabeth Swann—

4. Jack Davenport . . . Commodore Norrington—

5. Jonathan Pryce . . . Governor Swann—

Answer the following questions as you watch the movie.

1. Why is Elizabeth Swan told not to sing about pirates? Will bring pirates. Bad luck.

2. What is the name of the boy who is rescued from the ocean? How does Elizabeth know he is a pirate? Will Turner.

3. What is the *Black Pearl*? Ship crewed by the damned.

4. Why does Elizabeth fall over the wall into the water? She faints because of her corsett.

5. What is the pirate's real name? Jack Sparrow.

6. Why does Sparrow enter the Blacksmith's shop? He needs to get his irons off.

7. Why do the pirates want to kidnap Elizabeth? She is the governor's daughter.

8. What does it mean to "demand parley"? Demand a talk with the person in charge.

9. What does Elizabeth trade to get the pirates to leave? The golden coin.

10. Why does Jack Sparrow help Will get to the Black Pearl? Will's dad was a pirate.

11. What was the nickname of Will's father? Bootstrap Bill.

12. Why are the men of the Black Pearl cursed? Took treasure of Cortez.

13. What will end the curse? All the pieces of gold restored and blood repaid.

14. What makes the crew look like skeletons? Moonlight shows us how we really are—can't die.

15. Why is Anna Maria angry with Jack? He stole her boat.

16. If Jack was the past captain of the *Black Pearl*, why didn't the curse fall on him? He was on an island.

17. Why does Jack want to kill Barbosa? Barbosa stole his boat.

18. How does Jack say he escaped the island? Sea turtles made into a raft.

19. What did Jack use for a rope? Human hair.

20. Why didn't the curse lift when the coin was thrown in? Not Turner blood.

21. What is the monkey's name? Jack.

22. How did Jack really get off the island? Rum runners picked him up.

PIRATES OF THE CARIBBEAN VIEWING GUIDE—TEACHER ANSWERS PAGE 2

23. What does a ship symbolize to Jack? Freedom.

24. What does Elizabeth promise the commodore if he saves Will? She will marry him.

25. What happens to the crew when the curse is lifted? Barbosa dies. He gets his flesh back.

26. Who saves Jack's life from hanging? How? Will. Throws sword for his feet.

27. Who is in control of the *Black Pearl* at the end of the movie? Jack Sparrow.

Name _____

GROUP PIRATE SONG AND RUBRIC

You will divided into groups of four or five. Each group is to write a pirate song.

- The song must have at least sixteen lines—probably four stanzas of four lines each.
- The song must have at least four pirate jargon words or phrases included.
- The song should be written to a familiar tune of a song everyone in the group knows.
- Someone in the group should write the song on a transparency sheet to use to perform for the class. Get a transparency and transparency pen from the teacher.
- The group will go to the front of the room, place the transparency on the overhead, and perform the song for the class.

Names of people in the group:

	Weak (4 pts.)	**A**verage (6 pts.)	**G**ood (8 pts.)	**E**xcellent (10 pts.)
Song has at least sixteen lines				
Song has a familiar tune				
Song has at least four pirate jargon words				
Song presented on transparency				
Group Effort				

Total Points:_____/50

OBJECTIVES

- Students will become familiar with the historical radio broadcast from 1938, *War of the Worlds*.
- Students will compare and contrast the 2005 movie to the H. G. Wells novel written in 1898.
- Students will practice public speaking skills.

NOTES TO THE TEACHER

War of the Worlds (2005) is a very popular version of H.G. Wells' classic novel. Ray Ferrier has the care of his son and daughter, Robbie and Rachel, for the weekend. Ray seems to have some major communication problems with his son. Not long into the visit, lightening strikes the earth and creatures begin to emerge and try to conquer the earth.

War of the Worlds is rated PG 13 for frightening sequences of sci-fi violence and language. The film is 117 minutes long.

POSSIBLE PROBLEMS

This movie does have some strong language so be sure to preview it ahead of time. You may want to use a Guardian TV to filter out the language. There are also some graphic violent images and Rachel screams almost the entire film.

PROCEDURES

1. **Background Information**—Introduce students to the background of *War of the Worlds* radio broadcast from 1938 by using this web site: <http://members.aol.com/jeff1070/wotw.html>.

2. *War of the Worlds* **Viewing Guide**—Students answer these questions as they watch the movie.

3. *War of the Worlds* **Group Exercise**—Students will compare H.G. Wells' novel to the movie in groups and present conclusions to the class. Use this web site to get chapters of the novel: <http://www.fourmilab.ch/etexts/www/warworlds/warw.html>.

4. Use the rubric to assign grades to students' presentations.

Name _____

WAR OF THE WORLDS VIEWING GUIDE

Briefly identify each character as you watch the movie:

1. Tom Cruise .... Ray Ferrier—

2. Dakota Fanning .... Rachel Ferrier—

3. Justin Chatwin .... Robbie Ferrier—

4. Miranda Otto .... Mary Ann—

5. Tim Robbins .... Harlan Ogilvy—

Answer the following questions as you watch the movie.

Earth Under Man
1. Who has been watching the earth?

The Eve of War
2. Where is Ray's ex-wife going after she drops off her children?

The Coming of War
3. What causes the black-outs in the Ukrane?

Light Storms
4. What does Rachel say about the splinter in her hand?

In the Storm
5. What is strange about the wind?

6. Where is Robbie during the lightening storm?

7. Why do the cars stop running?

The Machine Emerges
8. Describe the spot where lightening struck.

Heat Ray
9. Describe the creature who emerges.

10. What is the "powder" that covers Ray's head and clothes?

Emerge
11. How do Ray, Robbie, and Rachel escape New York?

How We Reached Home/At the Window
12. What crashed into the house?

Name _____

WAR OF THE WORLDS VIEWING GUIDE PAGE 2

Human Toil

13. According to the newscaster, what happens when the tripods start to move?

14. How do the aliens travel to the earth?

15. What does Rachel see in the river?

Worst of Man

16. Why does Robbie want to get on the army trucks?

Exodus

17. What causes the family to lose the car?

Hudson Ferry

18. What causes the ferry to overturn?

Harlan Ogilvy

19. Why is Ray forced to let Robbie go?

Disturbing Revelations

20. Why does Ray sing Rachel a Beach Boys song?

21. Harlan Ogilvy says the invasion is not a war. What does he say it is?

Stillness

22. Describe the tentacles that come into the basement.

Days of Imprisonment

23. What do Ray and Rachel hide behind when the tentacles re-enter?

24. What do the "real" creatures look like?

25. How many fingers do the creatures have?

Alone with Harlan

26. What revelation causes Harlan to go crazy?

Under Foot/Earth Them

27. How does Ray get the tripod to release the captives?

In Boston

28. What are the "root" things Ray sees?

29. How does Ray figure out that the shields around the tripods are down?

Wreckage

30. Where does Ray find Robbie?

31. What causes the creatures to die?

REEL WRITING

WAR OF THE WORLDS VIEWING GUIDE—TEACHER

Answer the following questions as you watch the movie.

Earth Under Man

1. Who has been watching the earth? Intelligence greater than our own.

The Eve of War

2. Where is Ray's ex-wife going after she drops off her children? To Boston to her parents' house.

The Coming of War

3. What causes the black-outs in the Ukrane? Freakish lightening storms.

Light Storms

4. What does Rachel say about the splinter in her hand? When her body is ready, it will push it out.

In the Storm

5. What is strange about the wind? It's blowing toward the storm.

6. Where is Robbie during the lightening storm? Riding around in Ray's car.

7. Why do the cars stop running? The starters are fried.

The Machine Emerges

8. Describe the spot where lightening struck. The ground looks burned, but it is cold.

Heat Ray

9. Describe the creature who emerges. Tripod—a large machine with three legs.

10. What is the "powder" that covers Ray's head and clothes? Ashes of people.

Emerge

11. How do Ray, Robbie, and Rachel escape New York? They steal a car whose starter has been replaced.

How We Reached Home/At the Window

12. What crashed into the house? Airplane.

Human Toil

13. According to the newscaster, what happens when the tripods start to move? All communication stops.

14. How do the aliens travel to the earth? Lightening.

15. What does Rachel see in the river? Dead bodies floating.

Worst of Man

16. Why does Robbie want to get on the army trucks? Fight against the tripods.

Exodus

17. What causes the family to lose the car? The mob car jacks it.

WAR OF THE WORLDS VIEWING GUIDE—TEACHER PAGE 2

Hudson Ferry

18. What causes the ferry to overturn? A tripod comes out of the water.

Harlan Ogilvy

19. Why is Ray forced to let Robbie go? A couple is trying to get Rachel to go with them. He must choose between Rachel and Robbie.

Disturbing Revelations

20. Why does Ray sing Rachel a Beach Boys song? He doesn't know any lullabies.

21. Harlan Ogilvy says the invasion is not a war. What does he say it is? An extermination.

Stillness

22. Describe the tentacles that come into the basement. Long snake-like cord with an eye on the end of it.

Days of Imprisonment

23. What do Ray and Rachel hide behind when the tentacles re-enter? Mirror.

24. What do the "real" creatures look like? Flesh bodies shaped like the tripods.

25. How many fingers do the creatures have? Three.

Alone with Harlan

26. What revelation causes Harlan to go crazy? The aliens suck the blood out of people.

Under Foot/Earth Them

27. How does Ray get the tripod to release the captives? Hand grenade.

In Boston

28. What are the "root" things Ray sees? Alien food grown from blood.

29. How does Ray figure out that the shields around the tripods are down? The birds are perching on them.

Wreckage

30. Where does Ray find Robbie? At his grandmother's house in Boston.

31. What causes the creatures to die? They aren't immune to earth's bacteria.

REEL WRITING

Name _____

WAR OF THE WORLDS GROUP EXERCISE

You will be divided into groups of five. Each group will be given five chapters of H.G. Wells' novel *War of the Worlds* to read. Each person may read one chapter and then share information with his group. The group should compile a list of similarities and differences between the novel and the 2005 movie version.

Each group will share its findings with the class. The class will gain a good understanding of how the novel and movie compare and contrast.

Each person will receive a grade based on the part he presents with his group.

	Weak (4 pts.)	**A**verage (6 pts.)	**G**ood (8 pts.)	**E**xcellent (10 pts.)
Summary of chapter clear				
Similarities explained				
Differences pointed out				
Evidence of working with group				

Total Points:_____/40

OBJECTIVES

- Students will be able to define realism in literature.
- Students will be able to identify major themes of *Grapes of Wrath*.
- Students will write a five paragraph persusive essay about the movie's theme.
- Students will gain editing practice by doing peer critiques of essays.

NOTES TO THE TEACHER

Grapes of Wrath is about the Joad family who are forced to leave their land in Oklahoma during the Great Depression when the government forecloses on their property. The family is lured to California to become fruit pickers.

Grapes of Wrath is not rated and is 128 minutes long.

POSSIBLE PROBLEMS

None.

PROCEDURES

1. *Grapes of Wrath* **Background Notes**—Use this handout to give students information about John Steinbeck and the background of his novel. Use the *Grapes of Wrath* **Lazy Notes** to cover the information quickly.

1. *Grapes of Wrath* **Viewing Guide**—Students answer these questions as they watch the movie.

1. *Grapes of Wrath* **Quiz**—Use this quiz to asses student understanding of the movie.

1. *Grapes of Wrath* **Essay Assignment and Rubric**—Students write an essay about the movie's themes. Use the rubric to assign grades to students' writing.

1. **Peer Critique Questions**—Use these questions to teach the students to critique each others' work.

Name _____

GRAPES OF WRATH BACKGROUND NOTES—LAZY NOTES

Grapes of Wrath was first published in _____. John Steinbeck wrote the novel about a group of _____ who leave the Oklahoma dust bowl to travel to California to work as _____.

Steinbeck uses **realism** in his novels. **Realism** is the practice of _____exactly as it is. No attempt is made to glamorize it. We see the good and the bad. We see a "_____."

Grapes of Wrath was a _____ novel. The national banks back east foreclosed on mortgages of the farmers in Oklahoma after the_____. Men were victims of other men's greed. The government was no help to the victims. Steinbeck wanted to tell the Okies' story and to alert America to their plight. Steinbeck describes to America what he perceives as an _____ society.

Steinbeck believes that people are _____ and that the best in people will arise given the right circumstances.

"Grapes of Wrath" is a Biblical _____. The people leave Oklahoma to go to California, the Promised Land. But the Promised Land is only a disappointment. In the end, God will seek His revenge for the _____ people. "And the angel swung his sickle to the earth, and gathered the clusters from the vine of the earth, and threw them into the great _____ of the wrath of God" (Revelation 14:19). This hope keeps humanity alive.

Steinbeck also believes that all men are _____ through the spirit, kind of like the transcendentalists' idea of the "_____." As isolated families move out and join with others, they loose their family identity but gain _____ with other migrant families. They become part of a larger family, the _____.

The novel/movie shows the Joad family going on a journey. The family represents _____. The family is isolated at first. They experience problems and heartache, but the _____ prevails. They are changed and matured by the journey. They begin to look outside themselves to all of mankind. They become part of the _____ so that they can effect change.

GRAPES OF WRATH BACKGROUND NOTES

Grapes of Wrath was first published in 1939. John Steinbeck wrote the novel about a group of migrant farm workers who leave the Oklahoma dust bowl to travel to California to work as fruit pickers.

Steinbeck uses **realism** in his novels. **Realism** is the practice of presenting life exactly as it is. No attempt is made to glamorize it. We see the good and the bad. We see a "slice of life."

Grapes of Wrath was a political novel. The national banks back east foreclosed on mortgages of the farmers in Oklahoma after the Great Depression of 1929. Men were victims of other men's greed. The government was no help to the victims. Steinbeck wanted to tell the Okies' story and to alert America to their plight. Steinbeck describes to America what he perceives as an unjust society.

Steinbeck believes that people are naturally good and that the best in people will arise given the right circumstances.

"Grapes of Wrath" is a Biblical metaphor. The people leave Oklahoma to go to California, the Promised Land. But the Promised Land is only a disappointment. In the end, God will seek His revenge for the oppressed people. "And the angel swung his sickle to the earth, and gathered the clusters from the vine of the earth, and threw them into the great wine press of the wrath of God" (Revelation 14:19). This hope keeps humanity alive.

Steinbeck also believes that all men are connected through the spirit, kind of like the transcendentalists' idea of the "over soul." As isolated families move out and join with others, they loose their family identity but gain kinship with other migrant families. They become part of a larger family, the family of Man.

The novel/movie shows the Joad family going on a journey. The family represents mankind. The family is isolated at first. They experience problems and heartache, but the human spirit prevails. They are changed and matured by the journey. They begin to look outside themselves to all of mankind. They become part of the larger whole so that they can effect change.

Name _____

GRAPES OF WRATH VIEWING GUIDE

Briefly identify each character as you watch the movie:

1. Henry Fonda .... Tom Joad—

2. Jane Darwell .... Ma Joad—

3. John Carradine .... Casey—

4. Charley Grapewin .... Grandpa Joad—

5. Dorris Bowdon .... Rose-of-Sharon Rivers—

6. Russell Simpson .... Pa Joad—

7. O.Z. Whitehead .... Al Joad—

8. John Qualen .... Muley Graves—

9. Eddie Quillan .... Connie Rivers—

10. Zeffie Tilbury .... Grandma Joad—

11. Frank Sully .... Noah Joad—

12. Frank Darien .... Uncle John Joad

Answer these questions as you watch the movie:

Introduction

1. Where had Tom Joad been when we first see him?

2. Who does he meet on his walk home?

3. What has happened to this man?

4. Where has Tom's family gone?

5. What finally drives the sharecroppers off?

At Uncle John's

6. What does the flyer that Uncle John has advertise?

7. What does the grandfather plan to do when he gets to California?

8. What is Ma afraid has happened to Tom?

9. What does everybody think when Tom shows up?

10. What does Grandpa decide?

11. How do they change his mind?

Name _____

GRAPES OF WRATH VIEWING GUIDE PAGE 2

On the Road

    12. What is the feeling as the family starts out?

    13. All feel this way except for which family member?

    14. What is the first sign that things are not going to go exactly smoothly?

    15. What does Tom say he feels about the government?

    16. Who does Casey say he is praying for?

    17. What does the man at the camp say about the Joad's plan to go to California?

    18. How is the family treated at the gas station?

    19. What does the clerk do for the kids?

    20. How do the gas station attendants feel about the "Oakies"?

California, at the Camp

    21. What is the first thing the Joads want to do when they get to California?

    22. Are they successful? Why or why not?

    23. Where do they have to go (or else get locked up)?

    24. What is it like there?

    25. Why do all of the children come around their tent?

    26. Who comes to the camp in a car?

    27. Why isn't everyone thrilled with the man's offer?

    28. What does the sheriff do to the guy they call the "troublemaker"?

After the Fight

    29. What news does Tom bring back to the camp?

    30. What "good news" does the man in the car give them while they are broken down fixing a tire?

    31. Describe life in the migrant labor camp.

    32. After Casey is killed and Tom comes back, what is Ma afraid they have lost?

    33. Why does Tom say Casey was like a lantern?

    34. What does the nice work camp have that the kids haven't ever seen before?

After the Dance

    35. Why does Tom decide to leave, and what does he say he will do?

    36. How does Tom tell Ma she will be able to keep up with him and how he is doing when he is gone away?

    37. How does Ma say life is different for women than for men?

    38. Why does Ma say they will go on forever?

REEL WRITING

GRAPES OF WRATH VIEWING GUIDE—TEACHER

Briefly identify each character as you watch the movie:

1. Henry Fonda .... Tom Joad—

2. Jane Darwell .... Ma Joad—

3. John Carradine .... Casey—

4. Charley Grapewin .... Grandpa Joad—

5. Dorris Bowdon .... Rose-of-Sharon Rivers—

6. Russell Simpson .... Pa Joad—

7. O.Z. Whitehead .... Al Joad—

8. John Qualen .... Muley Graves—

9. Eddie Quillan .... Connie Rivers—

10. Zeffie Tilbury .... Grandma Joad—

11. Frank Sully .... Noah Joad—

12. Frank Darien .... Uncle John Joad

Answer these questions as you watch the movie:
Introduction

1. Where had Tom Joad been when we first see him? In the penitentiary.

2. Who does he meet on his walk home? Casey, the former preacher.

3. What has happened to this man? He's lost the spirit.

4. Where has Tom's family gone? To Uncle John's house.

5. What finally drives the sharecroppers off? The men on cats (tractors).

At Uncle John's

6. What does the flyer that Uncle John has advertise? 800 pickers wanted in California.

7. What does the grandfather plan to do when he gets to California? Eat all the grapes he can get.

8. What is Ma afraid has happened to Tom? That he's turned into a walking chunk of mean/Mad.

9. What does everybody think when Tom shows up? He busted out of prison.

10. What does Grandpa decide? To stay home—He won't go to California.

11. How do they change his mind? They get him drunk on cough syrup.

GRAPES OF WRATH VIEWING GUIDE—TEACHER PAGE 2

On the Road

12. What is the feeling as the family starts out? Excited and optimistic.

13. All feel this way except for which family member? Ma—She is having to leave everything behind.

14. What is the first sign that things are not going to go exactly smoothly? Grandpa dies.

15. What does Tom say he feels about the government? They seem to care more about a dead person than a live one.

16. Who does Casey say he is praying for? Folks who are still alive.

17. What does the man at the camp say about the Joad's plan to go to California? He has been there and seen it and there are too many people and too few jobs in California.

18. How is the family treated at the gas station? Like Beggars who have no money.

19. What does the clerk do for the kids? Gives them ten cents worth of stick candy for a penny.

20. How do the gas station attendants feel about the "Oakies"? They think they have no sense or feeling—They must not be human to live the way they do.

California, at the Camp

21. What is the first thing the Joads want to do when they get to California? Find work picking or anything.

22. Are they successful? Why or why not? No—There is no work to be had.

23. Where do they have to go (or else get locked up)? The transient Camp.

24. What is it like there? Packed with others just like themselves. All poor.

25. Why do all of the children come around their tent? They are hungry.

26. Who comes to the camp in a car? A man who says he is a contractor.

27. Why isn't everyone thrilled with the man's offer? A man who has taken work men like him offered before with no contract says they will take advantage of the workers and pay lower wages than promised because they know the workers are desperate for work.

28. What does the sheriff do to the guy they call the "troublemaker"? Shoots at him and kills a woman because he identifies the contractor as a cheat.

After the Fight

29. What news does Tom bring back to the camp? They are planning to burn the camp that night.

30. What "good news" does the man in the car give them while they are broken down fixing a tire? There is work picking peaches 40 miles down the road.

31. Describe life in the migrant labor camp. It is like a prison with armed guards to keep agitators out. Inflated prices at the company store. No one can get out at night.

32. After Casey is killed and Tom comes back, what is Ma afraid they have lost? Sense of family.

33. Why does Tom say Casey was like a lantern? He helped Tom see things clear.

34. What does the nice work camp have that the kids haven't ever seen before? Sinks and flushing toilets.

GRAPES OF WRATH VIEWING GUIDE—TEACHER PAGE 3

After the Dance

35. Why does Tom decide to leave, and what does he say he will do? He thinks the sheriff knows where he is.

36. How does Tom tell Ma she will be able to keep up with him and how he is doing when he is gone away? He will be all around, a part of everything that happens; wherever there is a fight so hungry people can eat, etc.

37. How does Ma say life is different for women than for men? Men live in jerks, when things happen (births, deaths, etc.) but women live life like a river that just flows on and on.

38. Why does Ma say they will go on forever? They're the people.

GRAPES OF WRATH QUIZ

True or False

1. Casey says he stopped preaching because he lost the spirit.

2. Grandpa says he can't wait to get to California to swim in the Pacific Ocean.

3. The family wants to go to California to become pickers.

4. When Grandpa refuses to leave, the family gives him cough syrup to get him drunk.

5. Ma is glad to leave her home in California and start over.

6. The troublemaker at the tent camp is shot and killed by the sheriff.

7. The migrant labor camp with cabins gives the family new hope for a better life.

8. Casey goes to prison for killing a deputy.

9. Ma says men live life in jerks and women live life like a river.

10. Tom leaves his family after the dance because he thinks the sheriff is coming to arrest him.

Multiple Choice

11. Tom Joad's family is originally from A) New Mexico, B) California, C) Oklahoma.

12. Tom's family leaves their home because A) they are forced to leave, B) Tom is in jail, C) they sell their land.

13. Tom was in jail for A) fighting, B) stealing, C) homicide.

14. How does Grandpa die? A) old age, B) starvation, C) a stroke.

15. Grandpa is buried A) in California, B) beside the road, C) at the first camp.

16. Rose of Sharon is A) Connie's sister, B) Tom's wife, C) Tom's sister.

17. The story takes place A) in the 1930's, B) in the 1940's, C) in the 1920's.

18. Tom's family leaves the tent camp because A) the government closes it, B) it will be burned, C) Tom kills a man.

19. The pickers strike because A) their wages are lowered to 2 ? cents, B) a man is killed, C) their wages are lowered to five cents.

20. Tom's family leaves the government camp A) to get more work, B) to hide Tom, C) because they can't afford it.

21. Tom says Casey was like a lantern because A) he helped Tom see things clear, B) he showed the way for change, C) he brought joy to people.

22. The clerk at the gas station sells the family A) Bread for 15 cents, B) nickel candy for a penny for two, C) sandwiches.

23. The children crowd around the Joad's tent at the first camp A) to beg for money, B) to be read a story, C) to beg for food.

24. Tom's face is bruised because A) an officer hits him, B) a crate falls on him, C) he fights with Connie.

25. The nice work camp is run by A) the farm owners, B) the government, C) the police officers.

REEL WRITING

GRAPES OF WRATH QUIZ—TEACHER

True or False

1. True
2. False
3. True
4. True
5. False
6. False
7. False
8. False
9. True
10. True
11. C
12. A
13. C
14. C
15. B
16. C
17. A
18. B
19. A
20. B
21. A
22. B
23. C
24. A
25. B

Name _____

STUDENT CRITIQUE SHEET

Name of person's essay which you are critiquing _____

1. Is the essay double-spaced using a 12 point font?

2. How does the introduction get your attention? Are there at least four or five sentences?

3. What is the thesis? Is it clear? Offer revision ideas if it is not.

4. What is the topic sentence of the first body paragraph? Does it support the thesis? Offer revisions if it does not. Is the paragraph developed enough? Explain.

5. What is the topic sentence of the second body paragraph? Does it support the thesis? Offer revisions if it does not. Is the paragraph developed enough? Explain.

6. What is the topic sentence of the third body paragraph? Does it support the thesis? Offer revisions if it does not. Is the paragraph developed enough? Explain.

7. Does the conclusion start with a rewritten statement of the thesis? Write it down. Does the conclusion summarize the main points of the essay and end with a clincher sentence? Offer suggestions for revision if it does not.

Name _____

ESSAY EVALUATION RUBRIC

	Weak (4 pts.)	**A**verage (6 pts.)	**G**ood (8 pts.)	**E**xcellent (10 pts.)
Appearance				
Introduction (development and strategy)				
Clear Thesis				
Body I (Topic sentence, developed)				
Body II (Topic sentence, developed)				
Body III (Topic sentence, developed)				
Conclusion (Thesis, summary, clincher)				
Sentence structure (Run-ons, fragments)				

Spelling (10 points, five points off for each error)_____

Grammar, punctuation, word choice, other (10 points)_____

Total Points:_____/100

chapter 20

Raining Retro

Singin' in the Rain:
Hollywood Musical

OBJECTIVES

- Students will learn the history of the transition from silent movies to talking pictures.
- Students will research topics from the 1920's related to *Singin' in the Rain*.
- Students will practice presentation skills.

NOTES TO THE TEACHER

Singin' in the Rain is a story about how Don Lockwood, his friend Cosmo Brown, and Kathy Selden remake a silent picture into a talking picture. In the process, Don and Kathy fall in love.

Singin' in the Rain is not rated and is 103 minutes long.

POSSIBLE PROBLEMS

None.

PROCEDURES

1. ***Singin' in the Rain*** **Background Notes**—Use this sheet to give students background information about the movie and the time period. Use the ***Singin' in the Rain*** **Lazy Notes** to give the information quickly.

2. ***Singin' in the Rain*** **Viewing Guide**—Students answer these questions as they watch the movie.

3. ***Singin' in the Rain*** **Group Research Project**—Students in groups research one aspect of the movie and present information to the class. Use the rubric to assign grades to students' work.

Name _____

SINGIN' IN THE RAIN BACKGROUND NOTES—LAZY

Singin' in the Rain is a _____. Adolph Green and Betty Comden were hired to write a movie using Authur Freed and Nacio Herb Brown's _____ written for the stage play the *Hollywood Music Box Revue* in 1927.

The film went into production in _____. Gene Kelly wanted the film to be primarily a dance film and insisted that his friend Donald O'Connor be given a part, so the script was revised. Kelly became the principle actor, co-director, _____, singer, and dancer. He had two new songs written to feature O'Connor's solo talents—"Make 'em Laugh" and the big _____ dance number performed with Cyd Charisse.

The film was changed from a _____ to one in which the story was tightly integrated into the songs.

Interesting Facts:

- Debbie Reynolds' _____ limitations caused much of her singing (the high notes) to be dubbed in by Betty Noyes.

- Cyd Charisse was hired for the big dance number because Debbie Reynolds could not _____ well enough.

- The big dance number with Charisse cost $600,000 and took _____ to film. They used three _____ engines to blow a 50-foot scarf that coiled around Kelly and Charisse as they performed an abstract ballet.

- The writers insisted on _____ accuracy for the portrayal of Hollywood's sound revolution. Original equipment or exact replicas were used for filming.

- Some of the tapping sound in Debbie's dancing was dubbed in by _____.

- Gene Kelly made _____ per week; Debbie Reynolds (only 19 years old) made _____ per week.

- Debbie Reynolds' most difficult number was "Good Morning." Shooting went late into the evening, and when it was over, she _____ because she had burst a blood vessel in her foot. She had to stay in bed for _____ before resuming filming.

- Donald O'Connor was smoking _____ of cigarettes a day while filming. After shooting the "Make 'em Laugh" number, he needed _____ of rest to recover.

- Almost all of the films-within-a-film sequences were based on actual _____ sequences. The costumes and equipment are exact reproductions, as well.

- The famous rain dance number was difficult to set up. A tarp covered the set to make it seem like night. The cover was lined with _____ to provide the rain. The rainwater had to be mixed with _____ to make it show up on film. Holes were dug in the street to form the puddles. Gene Kelly's suit was wool. It _____ as he danced and tried to coordinate the movements of his umbrella.

SINGIN' IN THE RAIN BACKGROUND NOTES

Singin' in the Rain is a catalogue film. Adolph Green and Betty Comden were hired to write a movie using Authur Freed and Nacio Herb Brown's songs written for the stage play the *Hollywood Music Box Revue* in 1927.

The film went into production in March 1951. Gene Kelly wanted the film to be primarily a dance film and insisted that his friend Donald O'Connor be given a part, so the script was revised. Kelly became the principle actor, co-director, choreographer, singer, and dancer. He had two new songs written to feature O'Connor's solo talents—"Make 'em Laugh" and the big ballet dance number performed with Cyd Charisse.

The film was changed from a catalogue musical to one in which the story was tightly integrated into the songs.

Interesting Facts:

- Debbie Reynolds' vocal limitations caused much of her singing (the high notes) to be dubbed in by Betty Noyes.
- Cyd Charisse was hired for the big dance number because Debbie Reynolds could not dance well enough.
- The big dance number with Charisse cost $600,000 and took two weeks to film. They used three airplane engines to blow a 50-foot scarf that coiled around Kelly and Charisse as they performed an abstract ballet.
- The writers insisted on historical accuracy for the portrayal of Hollywood's sound revolution. Original equipment or exact replicas were used for filming.
- Some of the tapping sound in Debbie's dancing was dubbed in by Gene Kelly.
- Gene Kelly made $2500 per week; Debbie Reynolds (only 19 years old) made $300 per week.
- Debbie Reynolds' most difficult number was "Good Morning." Shooting went late into the evening, and when it was over, she fainted because she had burst a blood vessel in her foot. She had to stay in bed for three days before resuming filming.
- Donald O'Connor was smoking four packs of cigarettes a day while filming. After shooting the "Make 'em Laugh" number, he needed three days of rest to recover.
- Almost all of the films-within-a-film sequences were based on actual silent movie sequences. The costumes and equipment are exact reproductions, as well.
- The famous rain dance number was difficult to set up. A tarp covered the set to make it seem like night. The cover was lined with sprinklers to provide the rain. The rainwater had to be mixed with milk to make it show up on film. Holes were dug in the street to form the puddles. Gene Kelly's suit was wool. It shrunk as he danced and tried to coordinate the movements of his umbrella.

SINGIN' IN THE RAIN VIEWING GUIDE

Briefly identify these characters as you watch the movie:

1. Gene Kelly .... Don Lockwood—

2. Donald O'Connor .... Cosmo Brown—

3. Debbie Reynolds .... Kathy Selden—

4. Jean Hagen .... Lina Lamont—

5. Millard Mitchell .... R.F. Simpson—

6. Cyd Charisse .... Dancer—

Answer these questions as you watch the movie.

1. In what year does the movie open? Where are the actors and actresses going?

2. Describe the "Fit As a Fiddle" costumes.

3. What are three of the stunts which Lockwood performs?

4. What is the name of the silent film Lamont works on?

5. Why isn't Lina allowed to speak?

6. Describe Lina Lamont's outfit.

7. What is the name of the first talking picture?

8. Who jumps out of the cake?

9. Why is the studio shut down?

10. What happens when someone pulls the mike wire?

11. Describe the problems of the "talkie" the *Dueling Cavalier*.

12. How do the actors decide to "save" the picture?

13. What is the new title of the film?

14. Who releases the publicity about Lina's singing talent?

15. How does Kathy Seldon get the credit she deserves for the picture?

Name _____

SINGIN' IN THE RAIN VIEWING GUIDE PAGE 2

Discussion: Answer in complete sentences.

1. As you watch the picture, describe the clothes which were popular during the 1920's. Be sure to include men and women's dress.

2. Which of the dance numbers did you like? Briefly describe three of them.

3. Look up this film on the Internet Movie Data Base (IMDB) and find out about any problems encountered in the filming of the movie.

4. Do you believe the musical is dead? Explain your answer.

REEL WRITING

Teacher

SINGIN' IN THE RAIN VIEWING GUIDE—TEACHER

Answer these questions as you watch the movie.

1. In what year does the movie open? Where are the actors and actresses going? 1927, Chinese Theater

2. Describe the "Fit As a Fiddle" costumes. Black checked suits, white hats, fiddles.

3. What are three of the stunts which Lockwood performs? Fights, falls.

4. What is the name of the silent film Lamont works on? Royal Rascal.

5. Why isn't Lina allowed to speak? She has a squeaky voice.

6. Describe Lina Lamont's outfit. Chandelier earrings, shinny head band, Ziff cheek curls, thick high heels.

7. What is the name of the first talking picture? The Jazz Singer.

8. Who jumps out of the cake? Kathy Selden.

9. Why is the studio shut down? Can't compete with the talkies.

10. What happens when someone pulls the mike wire? Messes up Lina's dress.

11. Describe the problems of the "talkie" the *Dueling Cavalier*. Can't pick up the voices.

12. How do the actors decide to "save" the picture? Make it into a musical dance movie.

13. What is the new title of the film? The Dancing Cavalier.

14. Who releases the publicity about Lina's singing talent? Lena.

15. How does Kathy Seldon get the credit she deserves for the picture? Let Lina talk and sing and open the curtain with Kathy behind it.

Discussion: Answer in complete sentences.

1. As you watch the picture, describe the clothes which were popular during the 1920's. Be sure to include men and women's dress.

2. Which of the dance numbers did you like? Briefly describe three of them.

3. Look up this film on the Internet Movie Data Base (IMDB) and find out about any problems encountered in the filming of the movie.

4. Do you believe the musical is dead? Explain your answer.

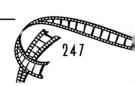

Name _____

SINGIN' IN THE RAIN GROUP RESEARCH PROJECT

Names of group members:

You will be divided into groups of four or five students and research some aspect of the movie. You will then present the information to the class in an appropriate manner. Topics might include such topics such as male dress, female dress, hair styles, dances, musical numbers, songs, actors, actresses, films mentioned, places mentioned, etc.

	Weak (4 pts.)	**A**verage (6 pts.)	**G**ood (8 pts.)	**E**xcellent (10 pts.)
Information seems accurate				
Information is presented visually				
All members contribute to the presentation				
Quality of performance (effort)				

Total Points:_____/40

REEL WRITING

Breinigsville, PA USA
23 March 2011
258282BV00001B/158/A